D1391145

746·920922 FAR

BARTON PEVERIL
COLLEGE LIBRARY
EASTLEIGH SO50 5ZA

NEW ON THE CATWALK
EMERGING FASHION LABELS

EDITED BY PATRICE FARAMEH

THE

WALK

INVITATION

PLEASE JOIN

FOR A SHOWCASE OF EMERGING FASHION LABELS

NEW ON THE CATWALK

INTERVIEW WITH SIMON COLLINS DEAN OF THE SCHOOL OF FASHION
AT PARSONS THE NEW SCHOOL FOR DESIGN NEW YORK CITY

PRODUCED BY

NEW YORK

CREATIVE COMMUNITY RSVP
WWW.EDAAB.COM

PRESENTING THE COLLECTIONS OF

INTRODUCTION

Fashion might be cyclical, but every so often the world is introduced to a designer whose work is so new, so emblematic of its time, that it changes not only the way we dress but the way we feel. What does it take to go from being a seamstress making individualized garments to creating a worldwide label that strikes a major chord? When we look to the past, we see the many talents that have managed to distill the zeitgeist, see into the future and alter the course of fashion. But who will be the new crop?

Simon Collins, Dean of the School of Fashion at the revered Parsons The New School for Design, has worked in all facets of this massive industry, from conception and technique to business and marketing to reach his current coveted position as guide for a new era of designers. In the following interview, Patrice Farameh sits down with him to hear what advice he has gleaned from over 20 years of standout experience.

So, what is it that turns a dress from a swathe of fabric into a transcontinental phenomenon, and a tailor into a visionary? Patrice learns that it is a perfect fusion of unwavering passion, unrelenting work ethic and solid insight. But in order to thread the needle an aspiring designer also requires some very surprising traits and carefully planned actions to lift him or her onto a world-recognized runway stage.

INTERVIEW WITH SIMON COLLINS *Dean of the School of Fashion at Parsons The New School For Design*

___ WHAT DO YOU FIND IS THE MOST BASIC TRAIT OF ANY GREAT FASHION DESIGNER? You must have a genuine vision and something important to say. There are those who can design a great collection for one season, but the next season they try to do the same thing again but don't have the same "special something." We find that the very best fashion designers have something to communicate through their work and are able to articulate that. Once I tried to get Junya Watanable to speak to the school and he said, "No, my work speaks for itself."

___ ASIDE FROM BEING HIGHLY AMBITIOUS IN COMMUNICATING THEIR VISION, DO YOU FEEL A NEW FASHION DESIGNER NEEDS TO BE SOMEHWHAT OF A SHOWMAN? A while back we had a conversation with Cathy Horyn who said she doesn't actually like it when people are very good at presenting—sometimes that gets in the way of their actual talent. If someone's really slick, it doesn't really go down very well with everybody. Of course, if someone's completely inarticulate that doesn't help either. If you cannot communicate your ideas without alienating others or without making yourself understood then it's not really effective communication.

___ WHAT DO YOU FIND ONE CONSTANT CHARACTERISTIC YOU FIND IN ALL FASHION DESIGNERS? If a person could be doing something else, they should be. Young fashion designers that come from our school could not do anything else but design. It is in them. They don't "work" because work implies something they don't necessarily like what they're doing. You never stop. If you want to make lots of money, you should be a banker. But that's not why you design. You do it because you have to. You cannot stop.

___ IN TERMS OF LUCK, DO YOU THINK IT PLAYS A BIG ROLE IN BEING SUCCESSFUL AS A FASHION DESIGNER? You're lucky if Julie Gilhart comes to look at your collection, but it's not luck if she likes it.

___ SO AS THE SAYING GOES, "LUCK IS WHEN PREPARATION MEETS OPPORTUNITY." Luck is worth nothing if you don't capitalize on it. And if you don't put yourself in the way of receiving luck then you've got nothing either, which is like networking by another name. The fact that one might run into somebody could be luck, but one must do something with that luck.

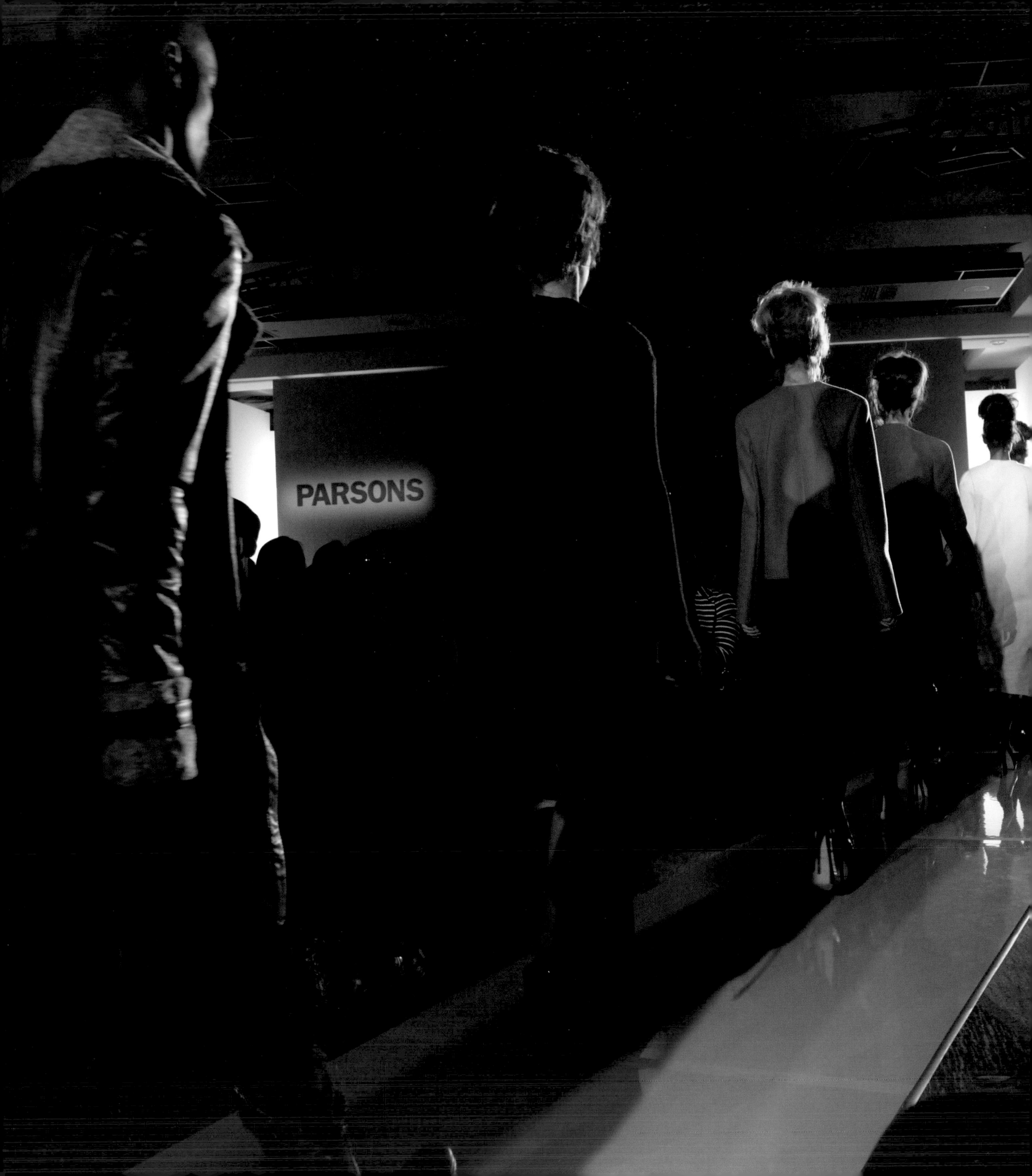
PARSONS

___ THE FASHION INDUSTRY HAS SO MANY DIFFERENT ASPECTS TO THE BUSINESS. WHAT ADVICE DO YOU HOPE THAT YOUNG DESIGNERS WOULD TAKE WITH THEM WHEN THEY LEAVE PARSONS? We always advise our designers to spend five to ten years working for someone else. Of course, many of those who don't eventually go on to become immensely successful. But we feel like learning your way around the fashion industry and knowing there is always more to learn speaks to the humility that we hope they always have. The opposite would be uninformed self-confidence. So many designers enjoy rapt attention early on in their careers from the media or from the industry. It's very easy to believe into the hype. It takes a long time to establish yourself in the business. Prabal Gurang recently spoke at our Benefit and one thing he said to our graduates was, "Fame is a result of hard work, a means to an end and not an end itself."

___ WHAT ARE THE MAJOR MISCONCEPTIONS ASPIRING DESIGNERS HAVE WHEN THEY COME INTO THE FASHION SCHOOL? It always interesting when alumni speak at the school and when asked how much time they spend designing they'll say "Oh, between resorts and fall, a weekend." The rest of the time is spent running the business. Designers in our school spend so much of their time designing so it's quite natural they would think they would go on spending all of their time as a fashion designer doing just that. Maybe when you're at the very top you can spend much more time being creative, or if you work for a big company then they just want you designing. But for many, particularly those who start their own business, the time spent designing is very small. As I mentioned before, what makes a great designer is that you've got a real message so you might not need that much time drawing; you might create a whole collection in your head just walking down the street.

___ WHAT IS ONE THING THAT YOU WOULD CHANGE ABOUT THE FASHION INDUSTRY? We are very keen to push sustainability in the fashion industry. We know it's not going to change overnight but every one of us can make our difference. And the more that we do it as a matter of course and not as an option or a trend, the closer we're going to get to acting in a sustainable way. We believe designers should be conscious of where things are made and who makes them and who buys them and what the product afterlife is: the consumer experience and the post-consumer experience. For instance, factories having healthcare and adequate education for children and producing garments at a level that can sustain that. So if there is one thing we'd like to change in fashion—indeed we are changing in fashion—it is people's belief in sustainability.

___ DO A LOT OF STUDENTS COME IN THINKING OF FASHION AS AN ART, AND DO YOU FIND YOURSELF AND YOUR COLLEAGUES GEARING THEM MORE TOWARD PRACTICALITY? We encourage them to do whatever's in them, but we also encourage them to be reflective and understand what they're doing. If somebody is designing for the runway and for the Costume Institute at the MET, we love that and we will absolutely support that. Alexander McQueen was someone who created the most exceptional conceptual pieces that you could wear on the red carpet, but you wouldn't necessarily wear out to dinner. He understood the difference between conceptual pieces and those you wear every day. Reflection is part of the process of design and we hope to instill that in our students.

___ WHERE DO YOU THINK CREATIVITY IN FASHION COMES FROM? I think it is innate; I don't think you can learn to be creative but you can learn to channel your creativity. I think there are a lot of people that are more creative than we give them credit for. I think as a culture we too often train people out of being creative.

___ WHY DO YOU FEEL FASHION IS SO ADDICTIVE AND ALLURING? You physically cannot avoid fashion. Unless you're living in Guantanamo Bay and you have no access to anything but an orange jumpsuit. But beyond that, we all wear clothes. Through the years people have said to me, "I don't care about fashion," but that's a mistake. They may not care about Vogue or the runway, but they care about what they wear because everyone has to make a choice when they get dressed. So, unless someone is literally dressed by someone else they can't help but be aware of what they're wearing. Fashion is just one part of that process. You could argue that someone doesn't care about architecture, because we don't get to choose where we live half the time, or they may not care about automotive design. We all dress up and often dress to attract other human beings and we know we do that whether we like it or not. Maybe that's just part of our plumage.

___ WHAT IS YOUR LAST PIECE OF ADVICE TO THE GRADUATING STUDENTS WHO ARE LOOKING AT THE NEWEST STARS DESIGNING FOR THE HOTTEST RUNWAYS IN THE WORLD? WHAT DOES IT TAKE TO GET A PLACE ON THAT STAGE? They have to ask themselves if they genuinely want to do it. If all they want to do is runways and parties, it's not going to happen. If they've seen it in the media and like the look of it, it's probably not going to happen. There's enough information out there to find out what a career in fashion is really like. They need to do their homework and figure out if it's really for them, and if it is and they're prepared to put in the work, then they have a chance to be successful.

ADA ZANDITON
LONDON

Bee-inspired "Colony" collection
Spring/Summer 2010

Ada Zanditon launched her eponymously named company in 2008 after being a finalist in 'Fashioning the Future' at the London College of Fashion. Ada made her catwalk debut in the Vauxhall Fashion Scout's "Ones to Watch" show in 2009 to enthusiastic acknowledgement.

«I AM GREATLY INSPIRED BY MODERN ARCHITECTURE AND ART THAT HAS AN ARCHITECTURAL QUALITY. THE SCULPTORS ANISH KAPOOR AND ANTONY GORMLEY INTEREST ME SPECIFICALLY. I WOULD SAY THAT THE CORE OF MY STYLE IS A WEARABLE SCULPTURE MIXED WITH AMERICAN FOOTBALL INFLUENCES.»

Her structurally-focused collections have the added integrity of using sustainable business practices. Her ethical fashion makes her clothes doubly beautiful, and allows the wearer to be part of the solution in both making (and keeping) the world a beautiful place.

«I AM INFLUENCED BY MY OWN WORLD AND IMAGINATION, CONCEPTS AND RESEARCH.»

While a previous collection sweetly sucks inspiration out of the honeycomb, her latest collection moves toward the birthplace of the scarab. The exotic and mysterious history of Egypt's Great Pyramids gives a profound thematic backbone to her "digitally printed dresses with sculptural detailing… that work from day to evening."

right, next page left and middle:
Bee-inspired "Colony" collection
Spring/Summer 2010

next page, far right:
"Pyramora" collection
Spring/Summer 2011

ALICE PALMER
LONDON

"Batman" collection
Fall/Winter 2010

Alice Palmer's mother taught her "the ropes" in knitting at the age of six. She briefly considered manifesting her constructive impulse through architecture, but settled on fashion design after making an incredibly flattering dress for herself out of a single ball of yarn.

«FASHION IS NOT SOMETHING THAT EXISTS IN DRESSES ONLY. FASHION IS IN THE SKY, IN THE STREET. FASHION HAS TO DO WITH IDEAS, THE WAY WE LIVE, WHAT IS HAPPENING.» COCO CHANEL

Inspired, she took a rigorous textiles training course at the Glasgow School of Art in 2000, and has steadily woven her way into fashion consciousness ever since.

«WHY DOES THE EYE SEE A THING MORE CLEARLY IN DREAMS THAN THE IMAGINATION WHEN AWAKE?» LEONARDO DA VINCI

Prior to launching her own label in 2008, she owned her own accessories company and managed a successful stall at London's Portobello Market while studying for her Masters at the Royal College of Art. The eponymous label has little fear of unraveling—Alice's head for business is just as keen as her fingers are with the knitting needle.

Alice stays true to Celtic traditions while at the same time finishing off each knit with a cutting edge. Her drive keeps paying off with accolades and awards: she was recently selected by John Galliano as one of three *Fashion Fringe at Covent Garden* finalists.

All pieces in the "Batman" collection are made from super soft merino wool

Alice Palmer *INTERVIEW*

___ IF YOU COULD DESIGN ANYTHING ELSE OTHER THAN FASHION, WHAT WOULD IT BE?
I would like to design a knitted piece of architecture.

___ WHAT IS THE BEST LESSON YOU HAVE LEARNED ABOUT FASHION SINCE YOU STARTED YOUR COLLECTION?
I've learned not to be influenced too much by what you see on the fashion runways these days. I've also learned to always keep my eyes open for new inspiration that you should never stop developing ideas if you want to create something truly unique.

___ WHICH THREE ADJECTIVES DESCRIBE YOUR COLLECTION AND FASHION PHILOSOPHY?
Sculpting, innovative and beautiful.

___ WHAT PERSONALITY TRAITS DO YOU THINK EVERY FASHION DESIGNER HAS TO HAVE TO START OUT IN THIS BUSINESS?
Determination to succeed, a strong sense of self-belief and a lot of patience.

"*IF I COULD DESIGN ANYTHING ELSE,*
I would like to design a knitted piece of architecture"

Spiked leggings were conceived as the ideal thing
to wear while riding the Batbike

Unconventional
bold KNITWEAR
with radical DESIGNS

BEC & BRIDGE
SYDNEY

"Smoke without Fire" collection with accessories
by Dinosaur Designs
Spring/Summer 2010

"THEIR DESIGNS DIVERGE HERE INTO A MORE RELAXED AND MINIMALISTIC AESTHETIC, ALMOST ATHLETIC CHIC, WITH A EXTREMELY VERSATILE LINE WITH EARTHY TONES."

"EPITOME
of YOUNG MODERN *CHIC*"

"THIS IS CAREFREE LUXE *at its best*"

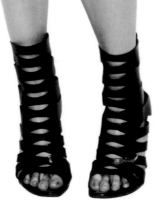

Becky Cooper and Bridget Yorston met at design school and from the first instant knew their acquaintance was destined for greater things. A shared vision to manage their friendship with a business partnership has led to a formidable force on the Australian fashion scene. Bec & Bridge strikes a fine balance between aspirational and achievable fashion, a niche its creators have worked hard to perfect since the label's inception in 2003.

«[OUR LINE IS] EFFORTLESS, SEXY, AND YOUNG YET STILL VERY SOPHISTICATED. MANY OF THE PIECES ARE SUPER VERSATILE AND LOOK JUST AS GREAT WITH A FLAT AS WITH A HEEL.»

A strong design aesthetic underlies each collection and resonates with their signature style—contoured lines and a sleek silhouette—the look is the epitome of young, modern and chic.

«BEC & BRIDGE KNOW HOW TO CREATE THAT SENSE OF EFFORTLESSNESS.» FASHIONISING.COM

It is the pair's meticulous eye for detail coupled with the ability to be commercially savvy with their designs that sets them apart from their peers.

left:
Bec & Bridge use a neutral base of colors to complement the ashen desert theme for their "Smoke without Fire" collection
Spring/Summer 2010

following pages:
"Violet Haze" collection
Spring/Summer 2011

"*BE A LOVER,*
be A TRIBAL NOMAD, *be* FREE SPIRITED"

CHRISTIAN COTA

NEW YORK

This collection was inspired by nature, technology and the Yucátan Peninsula
Spring/Summer 2011

Christian Cota's interest in the decorative arts compelled him to move to Paris and study fine painting before he returned stateside to graduate from Parsons School of Design in 2005. He launched his label in 2007 with an inaugural collection dedicated to what has influenced his artistic sensibility most deeply: the grace of nature.

«CHRISTIAN ATTRIBUTES HIS PASSION FOR FASHION DESIGN TO HIS FIRST AND GREATEST MUSES: HIS MOTHER AND LATE GRANDMOTHER. 'THEIR MANNER OF DRESS AND THEIR POISE WAS ALWAYS AN EDUCATION IN ELEGANCE. THEY DEFINE THE WORD.'»

Christian blends lush, organic forms that swoosh delicately around the body with exceptionally sharp tailoring that makes the toughest fashion critics take note.

«KARL LAGERFELD ONCE SAID THAT CHANGE IS THE HEALTHIEST WAY TO SURVIVE.»

Upon viewing this virtuoso's work, Style.com named Cota one of their "Ten Newcomers to Watch." In 2009, he received Fashion Group International's Women's Ready to Wear Rising Star Award. In 2010, the Council of Fashion Designers of America and Vogue named Christian Cota a CFDA/Vogue Fashion Fund Finalist.

following pages:
Collection inspired by Cubism
Fall/Winter 2011

Christian Cota *INTERVIEW*

___ WHAT IS THE BEST LESSON YOU HAVE LEARNED ABOUT FASHION SINCE YOU STARTED YOUR COLLECTION?
Women want to feel beautiful and my goal is to design clothes that make them feel that way.
___ WHAT IS YOUR FAVORITE PIECE OF CLOTHING OR ACCESSORY IN YOUR CLOSET?
My father's old Dior sweater; it is comfortable, elegant and carries the history of the man I admire the most.
___ WHOM DO YOU CONSIDER THE MOST STYLISH PERSON IN THE WHOLE WORLD?
A woman who is true to herself and relevant to her time.
___ IF YOU COULD DRESS ONE CELEBRITY, WHO WOULD IT BE?
I would love to dress Queen Rania of Jordan.

"OUR MISTAKES
AND IMPERFECTIONS
ARE WHAT FREE US
FROM THE BORING
AND TURN US INTO
THE INTERESTING."

CUSHNIE ET OCHS

NEW YORK

A double faced wool coat gets some edge from
glossy black pony skin panels
Fall/Winter 2010

Cushnie et Ochs provide sartorial assistance for braving that inevitable uptown/downtown cab ride every New Yorker must take. In a city of eight million, where did the designers find inspiration? The answer is in themselves, and their own cosmpolitan lifestyles. Carly Cushnie and Michelle Ochs are two Parsons graduates, who, joining forces while still in school, won the coveted CFDA scholarship, the SAGA award and Parsons Designers of the Year in 2007.

«CONFIDENCE AND A STRONG SENSE OF ONE-SELF ARE THE KEY ELEMENTS TO GOOD STYLE.»

With this impressive collection of top honors piled under their skinny leather cinches, Carly and Michelle went on to receive the best graduation gift any young designer could ask for. Even better than a diamond encrusted watch or a ticket to Cambodia, the young women were featured in a major Women's Wear Daily cover story.

«THE DIVERSE BACKGROUNDS OF BOTH DESIGNERS TOGETHER WITH THEIR STRONG SENSE OF FORM AND FUNCTION WITH PRECISE TAILORING RESULTS IN A COLLECTION THAT EXUDES SOPHISTICATION WITH A SIMPLE SEXY AESTHETIC.»

Blessed with such an auspicious beginning, it's no wonder that Cushnie et Ochs' clothes radiate confidence. They desire to show off the body yet also keep things elegant as they pay homage to classic designers such as Madame Grès and Geoffrey Beene. Cushnie et Ochs strike the perfect balance between metropolitan chic and metropolitan mettle.

left: Fall/Winter 2010
following pages: Spring/Summer 2011

"COMPELLING
TENDER-MEETS-TOUGH
COLLECTION WITH
SCULPTURAL SOFT
FABRICS MIX WITH EDGY
HARD-BITTEN LEATHER
EXTERIORS."

Luxurious furs of all kinds texturize
Cushnie et Ochs' warm winter coats
Fall/Winter 2010

Cushnie et Ochs *INTERVIEW*

___ IF YOU COULD DESIGN ANYTHING ELSE OTHER THAN FASHION, WHAT WOULD IT BE?

Carly Cushnie: For me it would definitely be interiors. It was never something I thought about growing up, but something I have been really drawn to. *Michelle Ochs:* I have always loved building things, so if not fashion it would have been product design.

___ MANY DESIGNERS TODAY SAY THAT FASHION IS A KIND OF STORYTELLING. IF SO, WHAT STORY WERE YOU TELLING WITH YOUR LAST COLLECTION?

Michelle Ochs: Creating a collection is very much like building a story and letting it unfold. For us, it was a road trip out west that inspired this fall winter 2011 collection. We imagined this sultry vagabond traveling across the American landscape… *Carly Cushnie:* … and this western traveler adventures into Native American territory.

___ HOW DO YOU FEEL ABOUT EXPERIMENTAL FASHION AS ART AS COMPARED TO THE FASHION NECESSARY FOR COMMERCIAL SUCCESS?

Carly Cushnie: They are both necessary; however, experimental fashion is not art entirely as it still has to function as clothes on the body. Art doesn't have to function because it hangs on the wall. *Michelle Ochs:* Commercial fashion is relevant because of the rapid pace that fashion moves in our world today. They are both necessary and appeal to different customers.

___"A SENSUAL COLLECTION,

for a highly confident woman who is both sexy and strong"

left: Spring/Summer 2011
right: Fall/Winter 2010

following pages:
Spring/Summer 2011 and
Fall/Winter 2010 collections

"Tough *urban* CITY CHIC"

"A kind of *gritty*
SENSUALITY"

DELIA COVEZZI

LONDON

*This entire collection was inspired by gladiator armour
mixed with a dash of Greek goddess*
Spring/Summer 2011

Delia Covezzi has cultivated a solid reputation as one of the best womenswear and accessories designers since graduating from Central Saint Martins in 2006. Following valuable apprenticeships at Stella McCartney and Tata Naka, Delia went on to design and produce bespoke collections for a range of top boutiques in Europe and the Middle East. After the success of this venture, she launched her own line in 2009 with immediate demand resulting from a loyal following and word-of-mouth.

«ALWAYS BE A FIRST-RATE VERSION OF YOURSELF, INSTEAD OF A SECOND-RATE VERSION OF SOMEBODY ELSE.» JUDY GARLAND

Delia mixes strong tailoring with feminine silhouettes, taking inspiration from the likes of Helmut Newton's Amazonian beauties and powerful historical female figures such as Joan of Arc and Cleopatra.

«HER OWN PHILOSOPHY TO FASHION CAN BE SUMMED UP BY A QUOTE BY YVES SAINT LAURENT: 'FASHIONS FADE, STYLE IS ETERNAL.'»

Delia wants women to feel both empowered and beautiful and what better way to do that than with clothes that are timelessly stylish but have a little added spunk? With sartorial nods to Greek goddesses, Egyptian pharoah queens and Amazons it seems that Delia has the right idea when it comes to muses.

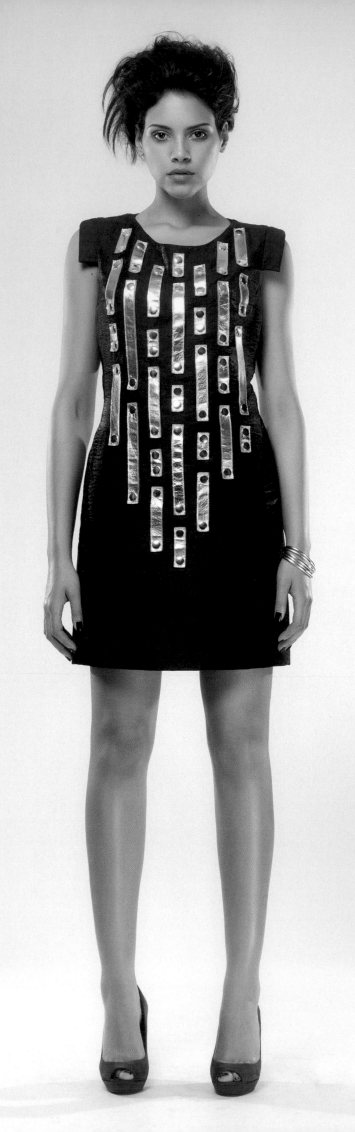

"TAKING INSPIRATION FROM THE LIKES OF HELMUT NEWTON'S AMAZONIAN BEAUTIES AND POWERFUL HISTORICAL FEMALE FIGURES SUCH AS JOAN OF ARC AND CLEOPATRA"

Delia Covezzi *INTERVIEW*

___ HOW DO YOU FEEL ABOUT EXPERIMENTAL FASHION AS ART AS COMPARED TO FASHION NECESSARY FOR COMMERCIAL SUCCESS?
Both sides need each other. Experimental fashion is incredibly important. It pushes the boundaries of what we consider fashion, both technically and visually. The commercial fashion feeds off and learns from this. It is a trickle-down effect. It is like this in all creative sectors; car design, interior design, art, music.

___ IF YOU COULD DESIGN ANYTHING ELSE OTHER THAN FASHION, WHAT WOULD IT BE?
A time machine... who wouldn't?

___ WHICH THREE ADJECTIVES DESCRIBE YOUR COLLECTION AND FASHION PHILOSOPHY?
Feminine, sophisticated and confident.

___ WHAT FACTORS DO YOU FEEL PARTICULARLY AFFECT YOUNG FASHION DESIGNERS TODAY?
Mass production, globalism and the recession; the retail industry is becoming increasingly generic, influential and brand-led.

___ WHICH DESIGNER FROM THE PAST DO YOU THINK EXERTED THE MOST INFLUENCE ON FASHION TODAY?
Yves Saint Laurent. Apart from introducing masculine tailoring for women, he was the first in 1966 to popularize ready-to-wear in an attempt to democratize fashion. He was also the first designer to use black models on the catwalk.

___ WHAT IS YOUR OVERALL APPROACH TO DESIGN?
Less is more.

" BODY ARMOUR THEME *to signify*
STRENGTH *with* PLAYFULNESS
and FEMININITY "

DORA MOJZES

BUDAPEST

"Roman Legionary" collection
Spring/Summer 2011

Dora Mojzes began to study technical design when she was awarded the prestigious ERASMUS scholarship from London College of Fashion. She completed her studies at Moholy-Nagy University of Art and Design in 2008 with a degree in Textiles. From there, the young Hungarian poured her imagination, which is full of sci-fi, historical and military references that any tom-boy can appreciate, into technically adept and feminine clothing.

«MY AIM IS TO CREATE THE IMAGE OF A 21ST CENTURY WOMAN WITH COSTUMES THAT SUGGEST SELF-CONFIDENCE AND RESOLUTENESS.»

Her graduate collection, entitled "Organic Forms—Futuristic Expression," won first prize at The National Association of Hungarian Artists. Dora's clothes give an aesthetic voice to strong femininity with bold cuts, patterns and evocative accessories. She draws from a wide range of stylistic influences, from futurism to classic 1940's Hollywood style to Roman legionaries, giving shape to post modern aesthetic values.

Pretty and tough were two adjectives thrown around repeatedly when designing the "Roman Legionary" collection

"ORIGAMI AS ORNAMENTS
ARE DORA'S TOOLS OF
FUTURISTIC SELF-EXPRESSION,
SHOWCASING A UNIQUE
AND BOLD IMAGINATION."

A futuristic sci-fi creature imagined
through the art of Japanese origami
for her graduating collection in 2008

"FUTURISTIC AND SCI-FI
things have always affected me"

H.R. Giger also served as inspiration for her graduating collection in 2008

EDWARD FINNEY

PARIS

Edward Finney enrolled in a fashion course at age 18 because he reasoned that he would be the only male in a room full of females. He soon realized flirtation was just one of many talents. So he moved on to Central Saint Martins in London. Though the gender ratio evened out considerably, Edward was content—he had fallen head over heels for fashion.

«IMAGINATION IS MORE IMPORTANT THAN KNOWLEDGE.» ALBERT EINSTEIN

Edward learned tailoring on London's Savile Row before moving to Paris where he worked under two of design's most gifted geniuses: Alexander McQueen and John Galliano. He directly assisted Galliano for four grueling but invaluable years, garnering enough experience to go solo in 2010. Edward initiates his rigorous design process with research and then focuses on the most inspiring details he can find. He teases out the aesthetic integrity of each garment through a series of comprehensive sketches, experimenting with fit, color and fabric in order to create an end product that boldly yet gracefully synthesizes extremes.

«FASHION TO ME IS A SENSE OF EXPRESSION AND CONFIDENCE THAT DOES NOT NEED TO BE HEARD JUST SEEN.»

Edward's impeccably tailored clothes recall enigmatic beauties like Marilyn Monroe and Mata Hari. His muses, like his clothes, radiate insouciant sex appeal and a devil-may-care attitude.

Collection inspired by Mata Hari
Spring/Summer 2011

following pages:
Fall/Winter 2011

"I CHOOSE WOMEN WITH AN INTERESTING STORY, SUCH AS THE EXOTIC DANCER, COURTESAN AND SPY MATA HARI, WITH INFLUENCES OF ANCIENT EGYPT AND PARIS IN THE LATE 1920'S."

"EACH SEASON IS INSPIRED BY A LEGENDARY WOMAN AND FUSED WITH A MIX OF CULTURES AND ART FROM AROUND THE WORLD TO CREATE A UNIQUE STORY."

Edward Finncy *INTERVIEW*

___ IF YOUR COLLECTION HAD A FEELING OR EMOTION, WHAT WOULD IT PORTRAY?

When I design I think of the emotions of my themes. This season was a lady that was powerful, ambitious, independent and giving.

___ WHAT IS THE BEST LESSON YOU HAVE LEARNED ABOUT FASHION SINCE YOU STARTED YOUR COLLECTION?

Fashion is a business and without sales I would not survive.

___ WHAT IS THE ONE SENTENCE THAT DESCRIBES WHAT FASHION MEANS TO YOU?

Fashion to me is a sense of expression and confidence that does not need to be heard, just seen.

___ WHAT STATEMENT BEST REFLECTS YOUR OWN PHILOSOPHY TO FASHION?

To make people look and feel great in the clothes I design.

___ WHAT FACTORS DO YOU FEEL PARTICULARLY AFFECTS YOUNG FASHION DESIGNERS TODAY?

It is important to find the correct investor that enables the young designer to grow as a viable business.

left: Spring/Summer 2011
right: Fall/Winter 2011

"PARISIAN LUXURY WITH
MODERN BRITISH DESIGN"

ELISA PALOMINO
LONDON

"Sacred Forest" collection
Fall/Winter 2011

Elisa Palomino began a passionate love affair with fashion while rummaging through her eccentric grandmother's house and stumbling upon all sorts of strange and exotic accouterments. From playing dress-up in the attic to getting a Masters from Central Saint Martins College of Art, Elisa followed her heart and it lead to the catwalk.

«THE ONLY REAL ELEGANCE IS IN THE MIND; IF YOU'VE GOT THAT, THE REST REALLY COMES FROM IT.» DIANA VREELAND

Before flying solo, Elisa worked at Moschino. Her already very refined sense of whimsy went well with the boldly irreverent style of this unique Italian institution. Afterwards she moved to Paris where she served as the Head of Studio at John Galliano and also collaborated with the Christian Dior's Haute Couture department.

«THE DRESS MUST NOT HANG ON THE BODY BUT FOLLOW ITS LINES. IT MUST ACCOMPANY ITS WEARER AND WHEN A WOMAN SMILES THE DRESS MUST SMILE WITH HER.» VIONNET

In 2008 Elisa left the "old continent" to become Vice President of Design for Diane Von Furstenberg in New York City. Armed with her valuable international and high-level experiences Elisa decided that it was time to give a platform to her own distinctive craft in February 2011, when she introduced her first gorgeous and exotic collection that is heavily influenced by the colors and prints of Japonisme.

previous pages and right:
"Sacred Forest" collection
Fall/Winter 2011

following pages:
"Eternal Spring" collection
Spring/Summer 2011

Elisa Palomino *INTERVIEW*

___ WHAT IS A MOTTO THAT YOU LIVE YOUR LIFE BY OR A QUOTE THAT INSPIRES YOU?
A quote from Claudio Monteverdi comes to mind, "The end of all good music is to affect the soul." I like to adapt the quote to: that fashion, in the end, should affect the soul.
___ WHAT IS THE ONE SENTENCE THAT DESCRIBES WHAT FASHION MEANS TO YOU?
Fashion is an everyday expression of beauty.
___ IF YOU COULD DESIGN ANYTHING ELSE OTHER THAN FASHION, WHAT WOULD IT BE?
Costumes for a Baroque Opera.
___ WHAT IS YOUR MOST FAVORITE PIECE OF CLOTHING OR ACCESSORY IN YOUR CLOSET?
Any one of my vintage flowers.
___ MANY DESIGNERS TODAY SAY THAT FASHION IS A KIND OF STORYTELLING. IF SO, WHAT STORY WERE YOU TELLING WITH YOUR LAST COLLECTION?
The legend of Persephone, the eternal spring and her descent to the Underworld.
___ WHAT IS YOUR FAVORITE COLOR AND WHY?
Antique Rose—it is really sensual and flattering on a brunette.

"THE END OF ALL GOOD FASHION…
should affect the soul"

ELISE ØVERLAND

NEW YORK

Elise Øverland's collections mix Scandinavian charm with rock and roll edge. In her youth, she aspired to be a professional slalom skier, but she has since shifted her competitive, daring spirit into sartorial undertakings.

«MY INSPIRATION IS MYSELF. HOW I LIVE MY LIFE CONTRIBUTES TO WHAT I WANT TO WEAR, AND WHAT-EVER SUITS MY LIFESTYLE IS WHAT COMES OUT. IT NEV-ER CHANGES. IT'S NOT LIKE I WATCH A SCIENCE-FICTION MOVIE AND THEN DECIDE TO MAKE SCIENCE-FICTION CLOTHES.» (INTERVIEW WITH VH1)

At Parsons, she began to develop what would become her signature style of free-spirited clothing that allows for fluid movement. This aesthetic proves to be perfect for several arenas. Aerosmith handpicked her for their tour wardrobe while she was still just a student trying to ace her exams.

«I USED TO DRESS MUSICIANS THAT REALLY MOVE IN THE CLOTHES… A STAGNANT PRESENTATION [DOES NOT] MAKE SENSE.»

Elise's open-minded dedication to her work continues to keep things interesting for buyers, fashion critics and clients alike. In a recent show she mixed her passions to great effect. Johnny Weir, the fashion-loving enfant terrible of the figure-skating world, skated around models wearing "sexy but wearable" icy pastels. It was the coolest show in town by far.

FELDER FELDER
LONDON

Daniela and Annette Felder are familiar faces on the British fashion circuit. The two German-born, London-based designers have earned themselves a British Fashion Award nomination, a cult following among A-listers and the highest caliber of retail stockists in Europe.

«WE ARE INFLUENCED BY MUSIC, NATURE, LONDON, THE TRANSIENCE OF TIME. A BIRD'S-EYE VIEW OF THE CITY, LAUGHTER, THE TEXTURE OF FABRICS, LADBROKE GROVE AND ITS PRIVATE DESIGN STUDIOS, MAD CHARACTERS AND ATMOSPHERE OF CREATIVE BUOYANCY.»

The identical twin sisters left Germany in 2002, traveling through Europe, India and America, working as models to fund their adventures. Eventually they settled in London, quickly securing internships with the hugely influential designer Robert Cary-Williams and milliner Stephen Jones. Both men inspired them to develop their own craft at Central Saint Martins and the conception of their own line.

«OUR CLOTHES ARE MODERN, EXCITING AND FEMININE BECAUSE PRIOR TO EMBARKING ON THE DESIGN OF A SEASONAL COLLECTION WE NEED TO GET REALLY INSPIRED, AND ABSORB THE GIANT CITY'S [LONDON] VOLATILE MOODS.»

Right from the outset, Felder Felder made its mark in London fashion, reinvigorating early-nineties grunge and successfully repackaging it into the perfect combination of structured shapes and soft layers, but in a harder rock and roll aesthetic.

right and following pages:
Fall/Winter 2011

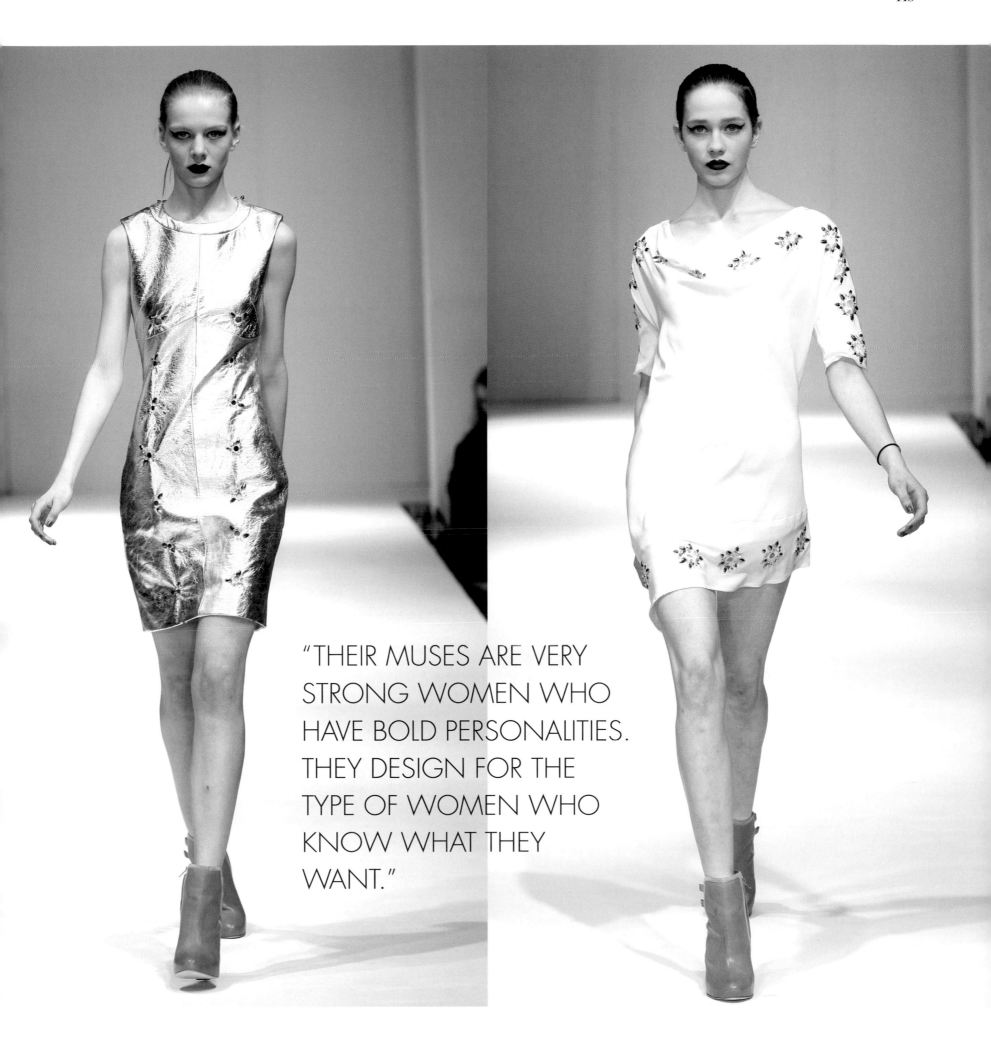

"THEIR MUSES ARE VERY STRONG WOMEN WHO HAVE BOLD PERSONALITIES. THEY DESIGN FOR THE TYPE OF WOMEN WHO KNOW WHAT THEY WANT."

_____ "ROCK AND ROLL CHIC
meets sensual and sophisticated"

left:
Fluff Jacket and Skinny Twist Pants
Spring/Summer 2011

right:
Wolf Jacket with Goat Hair and Lover Pants
Fall/Winter 2011

GRAEME ARMOUR

GLASGOW

Graeme Armour designs clothes that have all but scythed down the wheat from the chaff. His work is the wheat, as high-end buyers, elite stylists, and A-List it-girls can attest. Glaswegian born Graeme allows his fantasy to run amok in collections that contain a wide-range of idiosyncratic influences.

«GRAEME ARMOUR TAKES AIM AT THE HEARTS OF FASHIONISTAS EVERYWHERE WITH HIS LATEST COLLECTION BY BRINGING MODERNITY TO MOD LOOKS. THE YOUNG SCOT DOES BLACK AND WHITE WITH A TWIST, DRAWING INSPIRATION FROM THE DESIGNS OF GROUNDBREAKING 1960 LABELS LIKE COURRÈGES [AND BALENCIAGA].» JANELLE OKWODU (MODELS.COM)

For a past collection he took the idea of traditional Spanish flamenco and infused it with a futuristic edge, mixing ruffles with zipped leather and cashmere, thereby creating the beautiful ideal of a 25th century *Carmen*.

«ARMOUR'S CREATIVE TAKE ON MOTORCYCLE CHIC WITH LUXURIOUSLY LACERATED LEATHER AND FLAT RAZORED RUFFLES.» (STYLE.COM)

A more recent collection emphasized clothing as façade, so Graeme found inspiration in the flaps and cutouts of the butcher's apron. The true talent of the this erstwhile McQueen apprentice is what makes his clothes work in such a flattering way, and his intelligence allows him to wield his scissors and sewing needle with talented gusto, making sometimes unsettling sartorial allusions (butchers?) into irresistibly wearable realities.

"A SHARP EYE FOR CUT THAT EXPOSES ALMOST AS MUCH AS IT CONCEALS AND AN ATTENTION TO THE MOST ARTFUL DETAIL, HE IS THE FUTURE OF BRITISH FASHION."

ILARIA NISTRI
MILANO

Ilaria Nistri unfolds a universe of darkly futuristic fashion in every collection to date. Her first, held at La Bourse de Commerce, met with success in Paris in 2006. Her entire design philosophy is one defined by a constant examination into the non-natural balance of things.

«TRUE BALANCE OUT OF BRIGHT CONTRASTS AND CLASHING MATERIALS. VISION ENLIGHTENED BY CRYSTAL-CLEAR INTUITION.»

Ilaria creates heightened dynamic tension between a post-modern vision where rough elements, like leather and metal, and impalpable ones, like silk and transparencies, give life to unexpected beauty. The result is a fragile, poetic and gothic style whose color abstraction allows for graphic prints distinguished by a strict pictorial character.

«I DON'T INVENT ANYTHING. I IMAGINE EVERYTHING.» BRASSAÏ

Ilaria's land is inhabited by a conceptual she-warrior who protects her fragility. Deep femininity interprets cuts and instrumental deconstructions reveal manifold faces of the muse. In 2008, Ilaria was selected by Vogue Italy as upcoming designer and she reached the final stage of the Who is on Next contest called upon by the prestigious magazine and organized and promoted by Alta Roma. Numerous awards and accolades have accompanied Ilaria's illustrious rise to the top of the fashion game.

left and following pages:
Spring/Summer 2011

___"DESIGNING FOR THE FRAGILE WARRIOR;
a woman who fights and protects her fragility"

Ilaria Nistri *INTERVIEW*

___ DESCRIBE YOUR PERSONAL STYLE IN ONE SENTENCE.
Fragile, post-modern gothic, where rough elements like leather and metal combine with impalpable ones like silk and transparent fabrics, create unexpected moods.

___ MANY DESIGNERS TODAY SAY THAT FASHION IS A KIND OF STORYTELLING. IF SO, WHAT STORY WERE YOU TELL-ING WITH YOUR LAST COLLECTION?
The latest collection rotates around an idea of isolation, in seeking and defining a refuge that permits and protects an experience of intimacy. An isolation home, shell and protection for a non-place inhabited by voice-thoughts. A valuable experience: solitude with gilded walls whose voices are listened to by the angels in Wim Wenders' *Wings of Desire*. This is a collection with large hoods that close around the face like soft armour and structured collars that almost shield from view, allowing unexpected glimpses of light.

___ WHAT IS YOUR FAVORITE PIECE OF CLOTHING OR AC-CESSORY IN YOUR CLOSET?
Black leather trousers.

___ WHAT KIND OF WOMAN DO YOU DESIGN FOR THE MOST?
The woman I imagine is a fragile warrior: a woman who fights and protects her fragility, whose appeal emerges out of perception of who she is and her capacity to recognise and accept the various sides to her personality. A woman with intense femininity who gives fashion its most contemporary interpretation: a language that activates personal experiences and images. A tool for living and recounting the many aspects to her character.

___ WHAT IS THE BEST EXPERIENCE YOU CAN SHARE ABOUT YOUR VERY FIRST CATWALK SHOW?
My first catwalk, at the Milan Fashion Week, was not a runway show but a performance-event created through collaboration with the neo-avant-garde Italian theatrical company, Santasangre. Immersed in a surreal atmosphere, two performers trapped in a magic glass lantern interacted with holographic projections. Inside there were no real elements, only moving 3D images that created dreamlike, liquid, suspended settings, fully illustrating the concept that inspired the LIQUIDA MATRICE collection: a dark stain with coral flashes with a different slant each time. A pulsing cell, a planet, an eclipse, a life.

___ WHAT INSPIRES YOU?
An unnatural balance of things in art and nature, and also in people. This unstable equilibrium is the result of combining elements thought of and seen as distant, which allows unexpected ideas to emerge.

left:
Live performance catwalk event for launching their Spring/Summer 2011 collection

following pages:
Fall/Winter 2010

"ROUGH ELEMENTS LIKE
LEATHER AND METAL
COMBINE WITH IMPALPABLE
ONES LIKE TRANSPARENT
FABRICS, CREATING
UNEXPECTED MOODS."

left and following pages:
Spring/Summer 2010

JADE KANG
SEOUL

left and following pages:
This collection was inspired by the human body
Spring/Summer 2011

Jade Kang studied Fine Arts and Fashion Design and cut his teeth at the top Korean fashion houses before deciding to get expansive with his fashion outlook by traveling to London. There, at London College of Fashion, he added a European sensibility to his aesthetic. The result is a blend of diversified tailoring, futuristic urban femininity and contemporary romanticism that appeals to fashionistas in every country code.

«KNOWN IN FASHION CIRCLES FOR HIS WILD 'BIG' HAIR MASKING A DELICATE 'SMALL' EGO THIS EDGY DESIGNER TRANSFORMED HIS INNER REBEL INTO AN OUTER UPTOWN LABEL BY UNLEASHING HIS OWN DESIGN CULTURE IN 2007.»

Finishing in 2005, Kang's remarkable body of student work earned this young graduate the privilege to design a line for large commercial brand before going solo. Not only has his relentless talent brought him critical and commercial acclaim, he is also known for having a very rare quality in the fashion industry: modesty.

«I BELIEVE THAT FASHION IS NOT ART. IT IS DESIGN. AND FASHION SHOULD EXIST IN REAL LIFE.»

Jade's creations express a new urban retro-futuristic imagery that harks back to the visionary aesthetic of the Dada and Surrealist photographer, Man Ray.

Jade Kang *INTERVIEW*

___WHEN DID YOU FIRST BECOME INTERESTED IN FASHION?
I wanted to dress people to make them look beautiful, not weird or strange.
___IF YOU COULD DESIGN ANYTHING ELSE OTHER THAN FASHION, WHAT WOULD IT BE?
I usually get tons of inspiration from architecture when I design a collection so I would like to be an architect.
___WHAT OTHER THINGS INSPIRE YOUR COLLECTION?
I am inspired by digital art design and summer love.
___WHAT IS THE ONE SENTENCE THAT DESCRIBES WHAT FASHION MEANS TO YOU?
It brings challenge into my life.

JOANNA KULPA
VANCOUVER

left:
Spring/Summer 2009

following pages:
Spring/Summer 2010

JONATHAN COHEN

SAN DIEGO

Jonathan Cohen was born and raised in California to Mexican parents, but it was in New York at the Parsons School of Design that he found his aesthetic voice. During his time in and out of Parsons, Jonathan worked along various designers such as Oscar de la Renta, Doo.Ri Chung, Ashleigh Verrier and Patricia Field.

«JONATHAN DESIGNS FOR THE WOMAN THAT IS BOLD, ELEGANT, AND EQUALLY REBELLIOUS.»

His work is influenced by the multi-dimensional influences of sub-culture, construction, places and music. Whether it's the classic rock concerts his father took him to as a young boy, the bright and eccentric art of Mexico City, or the way the surfers in his hometown wore their wetsuits, each characterisitc presents itself in Jonathan's well-executed designs.

Jonathan Cohen *INTERVIEW*

___ WHAT WOULD YOU BE DOING IF YOU WERE NOT DESIGNING FASHION?

I can't imagine myself doing anything else. But my second passion is music. I wanted to be a songwriter and took voice lessons but I was terrible that I just let that go. I would want to be part of the music industry, maybe the business end, like owning my own record label. The starting point of every collection is "What is this girl listening to?" That always manifests itself into the attitude of the clothing.

___ DESPITE THE DIFFERENT STYLES OF MUSIC, WHAT IS THE COMMON THREAD RUNNING THROUGH THE JONATHAN COHEN GIRL?

I've been thinking a lot about that recently. I just read the Patti Smith biography and watched this documentary about different generations of female artists in New York (like Nancy Sparrow). I imagined a woman like that, whether she's an artist or she owns a gallery or is an editor. I pictured these women that are really involved in the craft of what they do and who are really passionate and though this might be cliché to say, but women who are independent. They can be with someone but they are still very much individuals and have their own sense of who they are. I always imagined her an artistic type, whether it's an artist, a poet, a writer or anything along these lines. She's complex, not an easy one to figure out. There are a lot of sides to her.

___ WHAT IS THE CULTURAL INFLUENCE OF YOUR WORK?

I grew up in San Diego and both of my parents are from Mexico City and I live in New York, so I have a range of women that I think about. She is someone who travels and sees different things. In Mexico the way people dress is a little more refined (like, no shorts) and more colorful. I've actually been to Frida Kahlo's house in Mexico City and her work has always had an influence on me, it's given me that boldness in color. In San Diego I grew up five minutes from the beach. In my mind that was normal until I got here and everyone was like "What?" That's where the relaxed feel of my clothes comes in, a sort of beachy casual vibe. So really all these cultural influences come together in my work.

"THE JONATHAN COHEN WOMAN IS COMPLEX, NOT AN EASY ONE TO FIGURE OUT. THERE ARE A LOT OF SIDES TO HER."

continued *INTERVIEW*

___ WHAT KIND OF MUSIC INSPIRES YOU?
For the last collection I was listening to a lot of Pink Floyd. They're very rock and roll but they're mellow. My dad listened to a lot of classic rock when I was growing up and would take me to Fleetwood Mac concerts and Aerosmith concerts. I know he sounds like this hippie druggie but he's not at all, that's just what he exposed me to. So I listen to a lot of classic rock. The Gorillaz totally inspired my fall collection. I just went to their show. Bobby Womack was on stage, Lou Reed was on stage: it was amazing! I grew up listening to a lot of Madonna so I guess that's where you can see the influence of my hard and soft, it's elegant but at the same time it has this edge to it that makes it rebellious. Going into the Spring Collection I've been listening to a lot of Hole and Courtney Love. *Live Through This* is a great album. And Nirvana. Empire of the Sun, they're like modern disco. So I have a huge range.
___ WHAT IS YOUR DESIGN PHILOSOPHY?
Colorful, it's obvious to say, but also elegant, rebellious and whimsical: complete opposites that come together.

KAROLIN KRUGER

BERLIN

The Hematite evening dress with draped sleeves
from the "Steining" collection

Karolin Kruger has carved out a solid reputation crafting modern, feminine, pure dresses that demand high quality and perfect workmanship. Nature with its inexhaustible variety of potential materials is her source of inspiration. These materials can be found in the handmade details that make her collections so unique.

«FASHION IS LIKE THE ASHES LEFT BEHIND BY THE UNIQUELY SHAPED FLAMES OF THE FIRE, THE TRACE ALONE REVEALING THAT A FIRE ACTUALLY TOOK PLACE.» PAUL DE MAN

She combines soft, smooth and luxurious fabric-like silk and leather to create sophisticated designs. Karolin makes her designs express the wearer, rather than the wearer being defined by their dress style. Made-to-order color choices address the individuality of each piece.

The Opal evening dress with draped back neckline from the "Steining" collection

«ONLY GREAT MINDS CAN AFFORD A SIMPLE STYLE.» STENDHAL

right:
*Sepeolith silk dress from the "Steining"
collection, with built-in stretch jersey body,
chiffon top with rock crystal seal, and double
train of chiffon and silk cêpe de Chine*

Karolin Kruger *INTERVIEW*

___ WHERE IS THE MOST UNIQUE OR SURPRISING PLACE YOU HAVE BEEN INSPIRED FOR MATERIALS OR PATTERNS?
There is not only one special place. It is always the whole nature like the forest, the open countryside, the hills or the ocean, which inspired me.
___ WHAT IS THE ONE SENTENCE THAT DESCRIBES WHAT FASHION MEANS TO YOU?
For me fashion is a form of art, which enables me to express my thought and feelings.
___ WHICH THREE ADJECTIVES DESCRIBE YOUR COLLECTION AND FASHION PHILOSOPHY?
Puristic, high quality, and sartorial.
___ WHAT KIND OF WOMAN DO YOU DESIGN FOR THE MOST?
My customer is a self-reflective woman who is interested in art and design. She loves simple, wearable dresses with a whiff of something special.
___ WHAT IS THE BEST EXPERIENCE YOU CAN SHARE ABOUT YOUR VERY FIRST CATWALK SHOW?
You need good organization and a perfect team for a successful fashion show.

"SOFT, SMOOTH AND LUXURIOUS,
fabric like fine silk and leather create sophisticated designs"

"*NATURE* with its inexhaustable *variety of potiential materials* is her *SOURCE OF INSPIRATION*"

KATIE GALLAGHER
NEW YORK

All images from the "Gris-gris" collection
Fall/Winter 2011

Katie Gallagher recreates the idyllic circumstances of her forest-fairy childhood in the cold, dark urbanity of counterculture New York, her vision thriving like lush dewy moss amidst the concrete outside of a dive bar. After graduating from RISD and working with threeAS-FOUR and Anna Sui, Katie developed a technical prowess that rivals that of a surgeon.

«EVERYTHING I MAKE STARTS WITH MY PAINTINGS, WHICH I'VE DONE EVERY SEASON PRIOR TO CONSTRUC-TION. I LOVE TO TRY TO RE-CREATE A THREE-DIMEN-SIONAL VERSION OF WHATEVER I'VE DRAWN; IT RE-QUIRES PRETTY UNCONVENTIONAL PATTERN-MAKING.» (ELLE.COM)

But her healing is of the sartorial variety; she is known for her desire to reflect the individual's soul, their "stories, personalities, moods, ideals and attitudes," into the structural body of her refined clothing. For Katie, fashion, when executed in the right way, can communicate with an eloquence more powerful than words.

_____ known for her desire to reflect the individual's soul, their
"*STORIES, PERSONALITIES, MOODS,
IDEALS and ATTITUDES*"

Katie Gallagher *INTERVIEW*

___ IF YOU COULD DESIGN ANYTHING ELSE OTHER THAN FASHION, WHAT WOULD IT BE?

I would design the interior and exterior of my own candy store. I would also design some of the candies and ice cream selections which would be sold inside. And no chocolate!

___ WHAT IS YOUR FAVORITE COLOR AND WHY?

I love to wear and design in monochromatic black or white. Since this is what I spend most of my time doing, monochromatic black or white must be my favorite color.

___ WHAT IS THE MOST INDULGENT ACCESSORY EVERY WOMAN SHOULD HAVE, IF MONEY WAS NO OBJECT?

An enormous black onyx ring. I know this isn't the most expensive stone but its certainly the most beautiful. If you wanted to rack up its worth, deck it out with some black diamonds.

___ WHAT IS YOUR MOST FAVORITE PIECE OF CLOTHING OR ACCESSORY IN YOUR CLOSET?

It's more of an outfit. Currently my favorite is my Victory Skirt in black from Spring/Summer 2011 collection, paired with a vintage 1990's Vivienne Westwood corset top in black and under the skirt my Center Leggings from my Fall/Winter 2011 collection. I also always have my bag from my first season hanging on my arm. It is made of laser cut leather and lots of gunmetal and black chain.

___ IS BAD TASTE LEARNED OR INTRINSIC?

I believe it's a bit of both.

___ WHAT PLAYS THE MOST CRITICAL ROLE WHEN YOU DESIGN: COLORS, FABRICS, STRUCTURE, OR SOMETHING ELSE?

One of the most important things to me other than the idea is patternmaking. Good design can't be justified by covering a sack with embellishments and crazy textiles.

KILIAN KERNER

BERLIN

"Leg Dich Neben Mich" [*Lie Beside Me*] *collection*
Fall/Winter 2011

right:
"Flieg zum Mond und bleib hier"
[Fly to the moon and stay here] collection
Spring/Summer 2011

following pages:
Fall/Winter 2011

Prior to becoming a designer, Kilian Kerner threw his heart and soul into thespian art, following in the great tradition of German theater at drama schools in Cologne and Berlin. The expressive psychological aspects of his background have had a clear impact on his foray into the material arts.

«THE BEST LESSON KILIAN LEARNED ABOUT FASHION SINCE STARTING HIS OWN COLLECTION IS YOU HAVE TO EITHER LOVE IT OR LEAVE IT.»

Turning to fashion at the realization that getting into character depended on costume, Kilian finds his greatest inspirations in mood, intuition and the powerful cosmic force of kismet. His instinctually designed collections evolve each season but always captivate by revealing just the right amount of emotion. He has shown at numerous Berlin fashion weeks and his ninth collection was streamed to an international audience via Vogue.com, placing his profound narrative pieces at center stage.

"CLOTHES REVOLVING
AROUND EMOTION"

"KILIAN'S DESIGNS TELL A STORY IN A MOMENT OF HIS LIFE AND ARE CREATED BY HIS INTUITION ALONE."

Kilian Kerner *INTERVIEW*

__ MANY DESIGNERS TODAY SAY THAT FASHION IS A KIND OF STORYTELLING. IF SO, WHAT STORY WERE YOU TELLING WITH YOUR LAST COLLECTION?

It's a story focusing on this certain moment when you are in need of calm and tranquility. "Lie beside me" tells a story about the year 2010 in my personal environment. It's about the joy of being in love, complete confidence and the experience of the suicide of a close, way too young friend of mine. These are those moments in which you sense yourself entirely.

__ WHICH DESIGNER FROM THE PAST DO YOU THINK EXERTED THE MOST INFLUENCE ON FASHION TODAY?

Hedi Slimane. He had great influence on a whole fashion generation and he is still reinterpreted.

__ WHICH THREE ADJECTIVES DESCRIBE YOUR COLLECTION AND FASHION PHILOSOPHY?

Sensual, self-confident, timeless.

__ WHAT IS THE BEST EXPERIENCE YOU CAN SHARE ABOUT YOUR VERY FIRST CATWALK SHOW?

The whole experience was beyond words. It was one of the most memorable moments of my life. In July 2008 I was presenting my collection at the Mercedes-Benz Fashion Week Berlin for the first time. Showing my creations in front of such a great and professional audience was very special for me.

__ WHAT WOULD YOU CONSIDER THE MOST DARING MOMENT IN FASHION HISTORY? WHO IS A MAJOR STYLE ICON IN YOUR EYES?

When it comes to the 1980's, for me it was definitely Nena. Everywhere you looked there were little Nenas running around. Even today they speak of the typical striped Nena pants and her characteristic earrings.

KRISTOFER KONGSHAUG

PARIS

left and following pages:
"The New Sex" collection
Spring/Summer 2011

197

Kristofer Kongshaug started his fashion career at age 16 as an assistant buyer for the Oslo luxury department store Voga. After working around clothes for a short time, aware his young heart skipped a beat when it came to fashion, his vision kindled like wildfire and in 2002 he began his studies at the Instituto Marangoni in Milan.

«ONE EARTH—ONE SKY—WE LIVE—WE DIE.»

Two years later he had become immensely interested in learning the construction of a garment in the most traditional and (to his noble sense of classic integrity) best way, so he decided to move to Paris and continue at the Ecole de la Chambre Syndicale de la Haute Couture.

«KRISTOFER LIKES TO THINK OF HIS WORK AS PIECES OF THOUGHTS, HIS ILLUSION OF LIFE. EACH GARMENT HAS A STORY TO TELL, EACH COLLECTION A CHAPTER OF A BOOK. THE DARK ARCHITECTURAL GARMENTS REPRESENTS SHIELDS OF PASSION, BODY ARMORS TO PROTECT THE SOUL WITHIN.»

Incredibly adept at construction by "moulage," Kristofer develops garments with strong lines and interesting volumes, full of precise detailing and painstaking craftsmanship, but at the same time entirely wearable. This Scandinavian artisan is a new favorite of fashion A-listers in the way he pays almost religious homage to the past while remaining totally in the present and forward thinking.

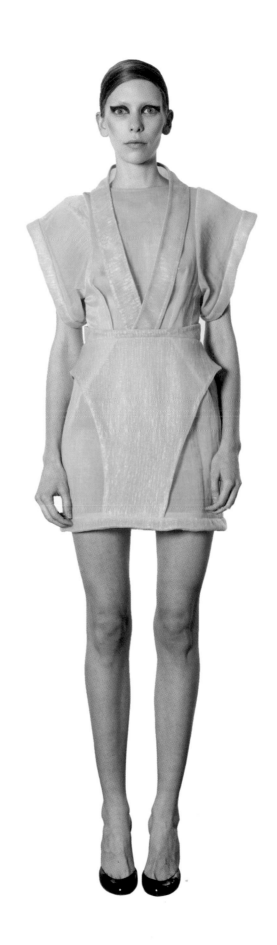

left and following pages:
"La Couture Mort: Agenda Caché" collection
Fall/Winter 2011

Kristofer Kongshaug *INTERVIEW*

___ WHAT DO YOU THINK WOMEN WILL DRESS LIKE IN 100 YEARS?

Do you really think we will get to experience 2111 as a human species? If we do, I hope we all are naked, dressed in each other.

___ WHAT FACTORS DO YOU FEEL PARTICULARLY AFFECTS YOUNG FASHION DESIGNERS TODAY?

Commercialism, everything is the same these days. Luxury went basic and High Street extreme, and everybody met in the middle and have created havoc for the consumers and buyers. What to buy when everything looks the same? It's chaos, but out of chaos comes new ideas and some ends, maybe that's what is needed in the mass suggestion we are living in.

___ HOW DO YOU FEEL ABOUT EXPERIMENTAL FASHION AS ART AS COMPARED TO THE FASHION NECESSARY TO PRODUCE FOR COMMERCIAL SUCCESS?

I don't. I think as a designer you should create what you feel, then edit it into something edible… things don't need to be commercial for success nor does an art piece need to be amazing. For me the importance is always that the garment is wearable, that there exists a chance that just a few people out there have been imagining this garment, and they need it to stop their hunger.

___ IF YOU COULD DRESS ONE CELEBRITY, WHO WOULD IT BE?

Cate Blanchett. I don't know why but she gives me this calm feeling. She's real.

___ WHAT IS YOUR OVERALL APPROACH TO DESIGN?

Make what I feel, another chapter in a book, a new character for the chapter, to evolve with my work and take it to new places. For me, it all comes from within.

___ WHAT INSPIRES YOU?

Almost everything around me, that's why you have to be selective, your surroundings shapes you. I have a thinking box I like to sit inside, all closed up with just a small glitch of light coming through a little crack on the side. From there I can observe emotions and shapes passing by on the outside, and clean my thoughts. As least that's how I imagine it would be if it was real. Imagination, a dreamscape of textures and buildings and human shells passing by, a little parallel universe only I can see.

KRYSTOF STROZYNA

LONDON

All images from the
Spring/Summer 2011

Krystof Strozyna already has six stunning collections to his young name after graduating from Central Saint Martins in 2007. While each line is kept interesting with evolving cuts, fabrics and inspirations, Krystof retains the integrity of his vision by always holding true to his favorite themes. The industrial aspect of his designs and especially his chunky, laser-cut jewelry lend each collection a structured strength that is crisp, efficient and never sloppy.

«POLISH-BORN KRYSTOF STROZYNA DESIGNS FOR THE CHARISMATIC AND SASSY WOMAN.»

Sharp cuts, monochromatic aside from bold splashes of invigorating color and special attention to an ultra feminine hourglass form, Stroznya manufactures modern sex appeal. His technique and talent have not gone unnoticed: upon graduating from Central Saint Martins in 2007, Krystof not only won funding from the New Generation sponsorship scheme, but was also invited to display his collection at Harrod's, the penultimate luxury store in London, as one of the winners of the Harrod's Design Awards.

"BODY-CONSCIOUS SHAPES, GRAPHIC CUTS AND OVERSIZED WOODEN JEWELRY ARE A FEW TRADEMARKS OF KRYSTOF STROZNYA."

left and following pages:
"Surati" collection
Spring/Summer 2011

LAKO BUKIA
LONDON

"INSPIRED BY THE
MINIMALISTIC,
GEOMETRIC SHAPES
ASSOCIATED
WITH CUBISM"

Lako Bukia's signature style—inspired by minimalistic geometric shapes and the Cubists—appeals to a woman searching for a new definition of beauty.

«FASHION IS A HARD GAME AND YOU HAVE TO PLAY TO WIN.»

Born in 1987 in the city of the Georgian capital city of Tbilisi, Lako gained entrance to the rigorous Tbilisi State Academy of Art where she took up Fashion Design and Textiles. She earned extensive acclaim for her first, charmingly titled collection "Mushroom," and was asked by the Ukrainian panel to show her work as part of both the Georgia and Kiev fashion weeks in 2009.

«CUBISM IS LIKE STANDING AT A CERTAIN POINT ON A MOUNTAIN AND LOOKING AROUND. IF YOU GO HIGHER, THINGS WILL LOOK DIFFERENT; IF YOU GO LOWER, AGAIN THEY WILL LOOK DIFFERENT. IT IS A POINT OF VIEW.» JACQUES LIPCHITZ

In order to continually be inspired and gain expertise in design technique, Bukia earned her second degree from the London College of Fashion. Her collections have been exhibited at Central Saint Martins in London and widely praised all over the world. Her innovative sense of fashion has lead her to work with Katie Burnett on several styling jobs in addition to having completed three internationally significant collections.

Lako Bukia *INTERVIEW*

___ IF YOU COULD DESIGN ANYTHING ELSE OTHER THAN FASHION, WHAT WOULD IT BE?

Collecting toys is one of my hobbies. I love being in Hamleys and playing around. My mum always thought I would eventually connect my hobby to my work. So I guess if I was not a designer of clothes, I would definitely be a designer or the maker of the toys.

___ IF YOU COULD DRESS ONE CELEBRITY, WHO WOULD IT BE?

For me being just beautiful is not enough, you inner self matters just as much. One has to be not only beautiful but also interesting to become inspiration. That's why I think Natalie Portman is the person I would love to dress. She is beautiful as well as an amazing actress but most importantly she has a special, intelligent character.

___ WHOM DO YOU CONSIDER THE MOST STYLISH PERSON IN THE WHOLE WORLD?

I considered Audrey Hepburn at first. She was the style icon, but now it is Anna Dello Russo, the editor and creative consultant for *Vogue Japan*.

___ WHAT WILL YOU BE ADDING TO YOUR OWN WARDROBE THIS SPRING?

Hopefully I will be adding a lot of my own designed clothes; I never have time to design for myself. Hopefully this time it will happen. And of course, my favorite Celine handbag.

___ WHAT IS YOUR MOST FAVORITE PIECE OF CLOTHING OR ACCESSORY IN YOUR CLOSET?

I collect jewelry and I am in love with all the pieces I have. The reason behind my obsession I think could be the fact that I, myself, do not know how to design and make jewelry. If I had to choose my favorite peace, little 'L' initial is the most important one; it was gifted to me by my mother. It is a white gold charm with small diamonds that I always wear.

___ WHAT IS THE GREATEST INDULGENT ACCESSORY EVERY WOMAN SHOULD HAVE, IF MONEY WAS NO OBJECT?

Agent Provocateur underwear.

The "Surati" collection was inspired by traditional Georgian architecture

LIMI FEU
TOKYO

This entire collection was inspired by matrimony
Spring/Summer 2011

Limi Feu taps into her deep stores of genetically passed down talent to create clothes for her own generation. The Limi Feu style is an evolved form of hybridization. Her father, Yohji Yamamoto, is a master of Japanese fashion. It is clear from Limi's innovative creativity that he has produced a more than worthy heiress to lead the new wave of avant garde designers from the East.

«AS A WOMAN, LIMI DESIGNS REAL CLOTHES FOR REAL WOMEN, NOT AN IDEAL.» (VIRTUALJAPAN.COM)

Androgyny with a formal twist and billowing beautifully executed shapes mix the old with the new. Where her father was a romantic, Limi, who took the last name Feu from the French word for "fire," has a wilder side. She takes from her lineage the excellent skills of tailoring but raises the tempurature with rock and roll and punk.

MANDY COON
NEW YORK

left: Fall/Winter 2010

following pages:
Collection inspired by jellyfish
Spring/Summer 2011

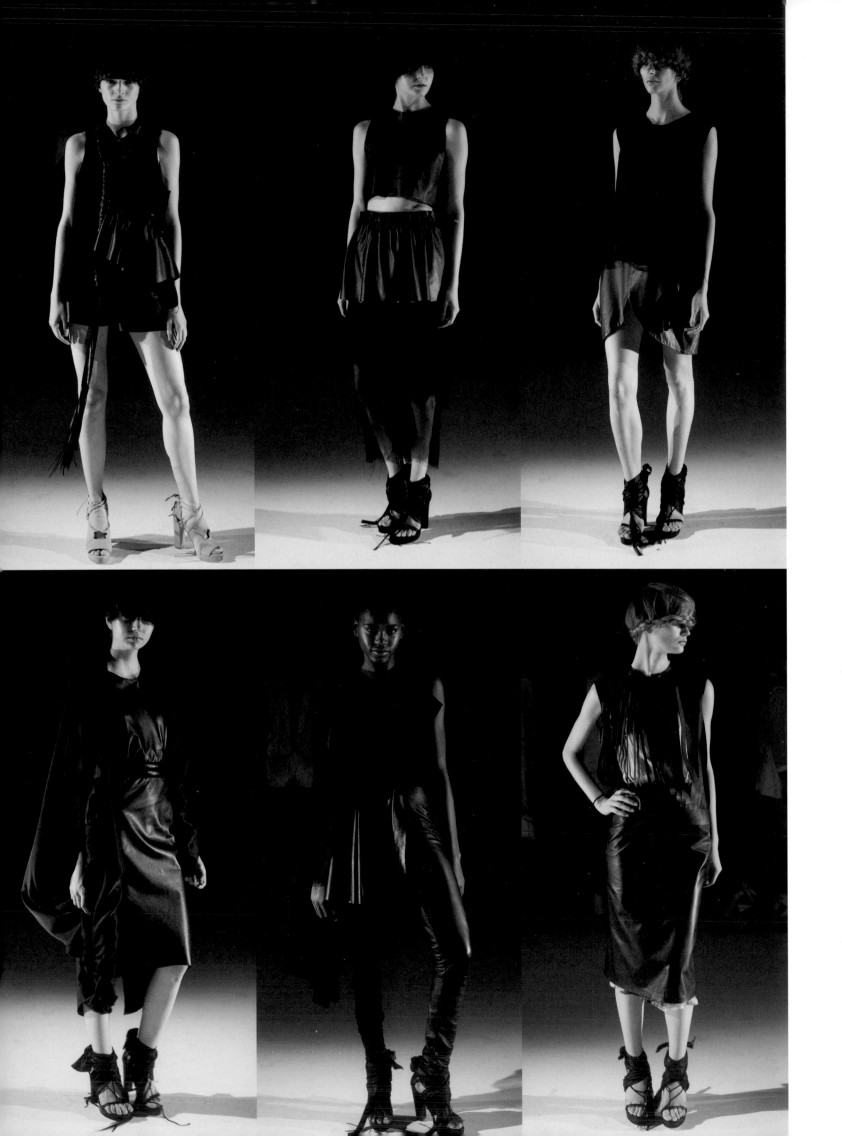

Mandy Coon was thrust into the fashion world at age 20 when approached by a model scout at a Houston, Texas shopping mall. This blue-eyed beauty spent years being fitted for clothes, fostering in her a deep and personal appreciation for garment construction as well as a very eclectic personal style.

«HER GEOMETRICAL CLOTHING EXUDES A MASCULINE/FEMININE, EDGY/SOFT DUALITY ALLOWING IT TO TRAVERSE THE UPTOWN/DOWNTOWN DIVIDE WITH EASE.»

After trying her hand at several fashion projects and collaborations, Mandy fell in love with being on the other side of the catwalk, delving further into her knowledge of the industry by learning valuable techniques in haute couture sewing and tailoring at the Fashion Institute of Technology located in the heart of New York City's Garment District. She soon landed an apprenticeship with Danish designer Camilla Stærk, where she put her skills to use to create handmade runway pieces.

«WHAT'S ESPECIALLY APPEALING ABOUT COON IS HER WILLINGNESS TO BE AD HOC. YOU CAN PRACTICALLY WATCH THE CREATIVE PROCESS UNFOLD ON HER CLOTHES.» (STYLE.COM)

In 2010 she launched her own brand that has become known for melding meticulous details with intriguing functionality. Coon resides in the East Village and credits her French bulldog Petunia as an endless source of inspiration.

right and following pages:
Fall/Winter 2010

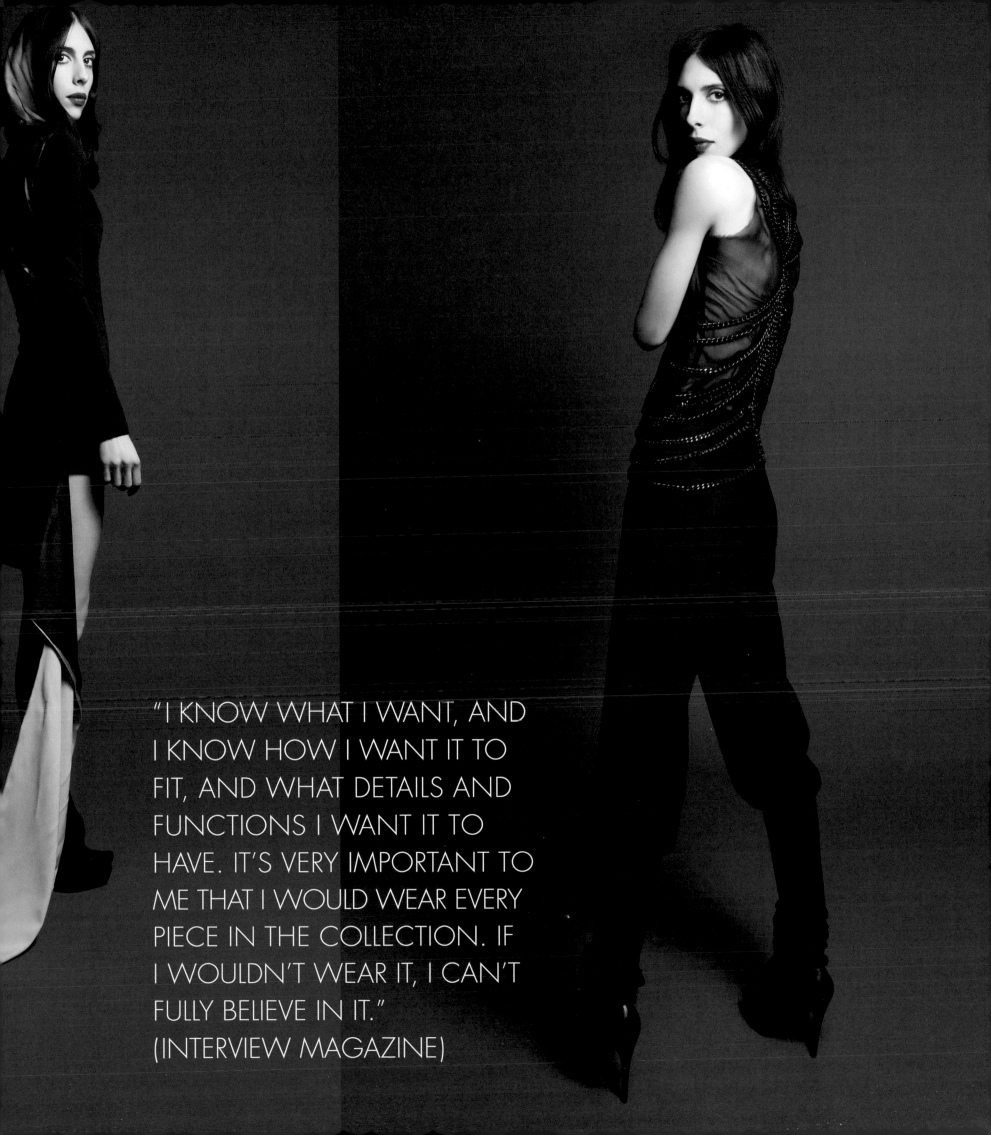

"I KNOW WHAT I WANT, AND
I KNOW HOW I WANT IT TO
FIT, AND WHAT DETAILS AND
FUNCTIONS I WANT IT TO
HAVE. IT'S VERY IMPORTANT TO
ME THAT I WOULD WEAR EVERY
PIECE IN THE COLLECTION. IF
I WOULDN'T WEAR IT, I CAN'T
FULLY BELIEVE IN IT."
(INTERVIEW MAGAZINE)

Mandy Coon *INTERVIEW*

___ WHAT IS YOUR OVERALL APPROACH TO DESIGN?
I try not to censor myself and go with my instincts.
___ WHERE IS THE MOST UNIQUE OR SURPRISING PLACE YOU HAVE BEEN INSPIRED FOR MATERIALS OR PATTERNS?
Jellyfish!
___ WHEN DID YOU FIRST BECOME INTERESTED IN FASHION?
Reading my mother's issues of *Vogue* as a little girl.
___ IF YOU COULD DESIGN ANYTHING ELSE OTHER THAN FASHION, WHAT WOULD IT BE?
I would love to design furniture.
___ THREE WORDS TO DESCRIBE YOUR STYLE?
Structural, playful and textural.
___ WHAT IS THE KEY ELEMENT FOR GOOD FASHION SENSE AND STYLE?
One should feel comfortable in what they are wearing. If you don't feel comfortable, it shows.
___ WHAT WOULD YOU CONSIDER THE MOST DARING MOMENT IN FASHION HISTORY?
The Schiaparelli skeleton dress was scandalous, daring and so ahead of its time.

"I WAS WATCHING THE FILM 'SOME CAME RUNNING', AND SHIRLEY MACLAINE'S CHARACTER CARRIES AROUND A RATTY, BEATEN UP STUFFED RABBIT FOR THE ENTIRE MOVIE THAT IS ACTUALLY A PURSE. SHE'S CONSTANTLY UNZIPPING IT AND POWDERING HER NOSE. I BECAME OBSESSED AND DECIDED I NEEDED TO MAKE A LEATHER BUNNY."
(THEBLOCK-MAG.COM)

MARKO MITANOVSKI

LONDON

This entire collection was inspired by Lady Macbeth
Spring/Summer 2010

Marko Mitanovski is a London-based Serbian designer who graduated from the College of Design in Belgrade in 2009. He was one of the chosen designers on for the "Ones to Watch" show that was held at London Fashion Week in September 2009. It was an open competition for young designers and he was one of only four designers that were invited to take part.

«I WAS INSPIRED BY ELEMENTS OF RENAISSANCE COSTUME, WHICH I EXPERIMENTED WITH. I EXAGGERATED AND TRANSPIRED COLLARS IN SEVERAL WAYS BY PLEATING ECO LEATHER, TO HONOUR THE SILHOUETTE OF THE COSTUME—THE COLLECTION IS NOT AN INTEGRAL VISION OF ELIZABETHAN COSTUME, BUT ITS REPLICA OF THE BASIC THEME.»

Following swooning praise from the press, outstanding awards and popularity among fashion-forward A-list celebrities like Lady Gaga, Marko launched his line.

«MY APPROACH TO FASHION IS VERY ARTISTIC. IT'S NOT MUCH ABOUT THE TRENDS OR SOMETHING THAT IS COMMERCIAL THAT YOU CAN WEAR EVERY DAY. I LIKE TO DO CONCEPTUALS. SO THE STORY THAT IS BEHIND MY COLLECTION IS VERY IMPORTANT TO ME.» (TIME OUT CHICAGO)

His clothes are sculptural and theatrical in form, employing detailed construction and precise geometry for a daring aesthetic. His inspirations anchor his designs in appealing erudition—his most recent collection was based on Lady Macbeth. The collection had its basis in the structural form of Renaissance costume but was exaggerated and added to with fetish and punk, thus carrying the Elizabethan era directly into subcultures of the 21st century.

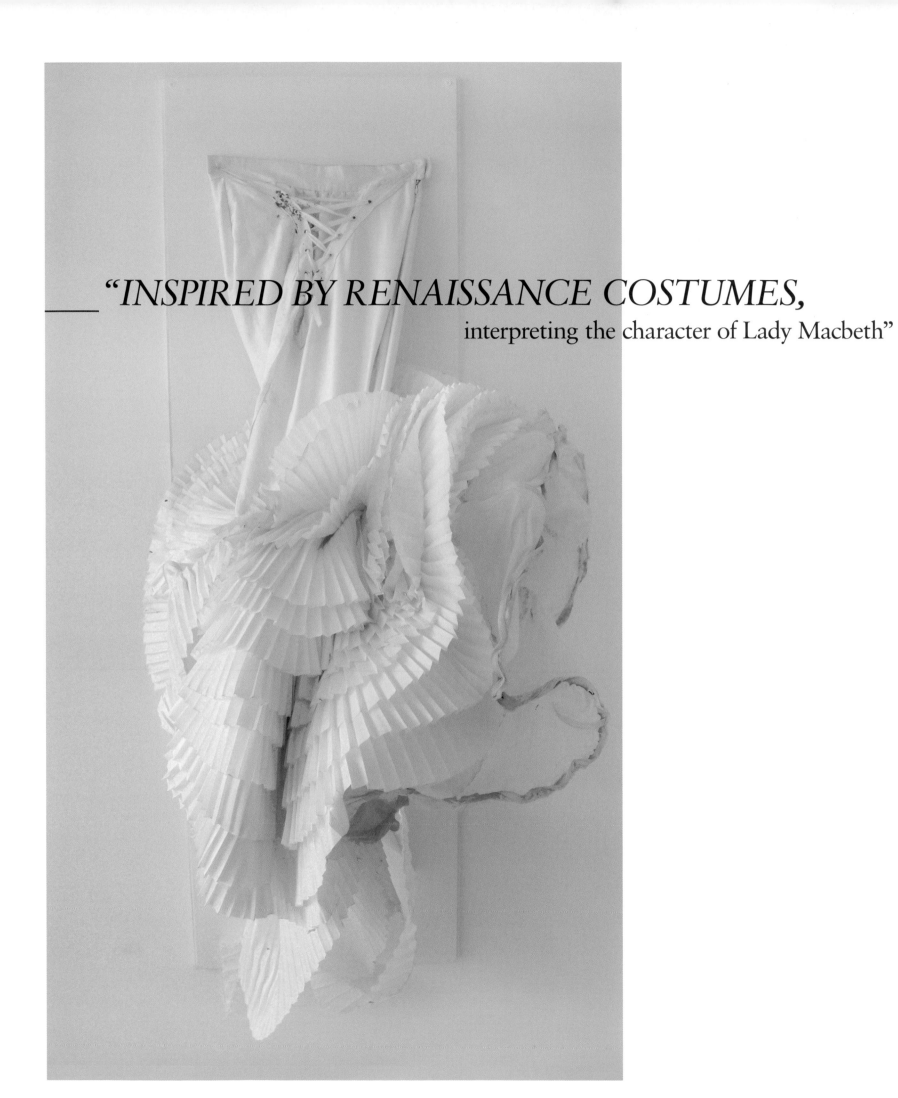

"INSPIRED BY RENAISSANCE COSTUMES,
interpreting the character of Lady Macbeth"

"…HYBRID OF THE SEXY COMPLEX SILHOUETTES OF THE SHAKESPEARIAN ERA AND A MODERN TRAGEDY IN A POST APOCOLYPTIC WORLD"

"BOLD GRAPHICS,
a hyperrealist aesthetic and industrial jewelry"

left and following pages:
This collection was inspired by interiors
Spring/Summer 2011

this page:
Spring/Summer 2010

Mary Katrantzou attended the Rhode Island School of Design and then completed both her BA and MA at Central Saint Martins. After assisting fellow Athenian Sophia Kokosalaki and freelancing for Bill Blass, amongst other designers, Mary began her own line which expresses her strong creative concepts.

«WITH THIS COLLECTION I WANTED TO PUT THE ROOM ON THE WOMAN, RATHER THAN THE WOMAN IN THE ROOM.»

Domesticity aside, even if the woman were in a room in one of her designs she would stand out. Mary's bold prints are playful, colorful and intelligently whimsical, her tailoring excellent and innovative, and her philosophy neo-surrealistic.

"PLAYFUL, COLORFUL …

…INTELLIGENTLY WHIMSICAL"

left:
Fall/Winter 2009
right:
Spring/Summer 2010

following pages: *This collection was
inspired by 18th century society paintings*
Fall/Winter 2010

"PRINT IS PUSHED ABOVE
AND BEYOND WHERE
WE HAVE SEEN IT GO
BEFORE, CLASHING AND
CONTRASTING, ACROSS
GARMENTS, OVERWHELMING
THE VIEWER, BUT NEVER THE
WEARER." ALEX FURY

MATTEO THIELA

MILAN

All images are from the 2010 "Retexo" collection

"THE COLOR THAT ALWAYS HAS POWER TO ME IS RED, IT EXPANDS MY FEELINGS AND GIVES ME ENERGY."

Matteo Thiela was born in Milan in 1972 and currently resides in a city steeped in two worlds. Turin has all the inspiring natural beauty of surrounding mountains as well as the energy of a major industrial component. The rich history of Italian manufacturing and appreciation for beauty has always been a major factor in Matteo's approach to design.

«SENSUALITY FOR ME IS LIKE CLASS PEOPLE HAVE IN-SIDE. A DRESS MUST BE ART FOR AN ARTIST.»

Working at myriad Italian fashion houses, Matteo gained expert skills at tailoring and concept design that resulted in his winning the prestigious Limoni Freshon First Prize as well as having his work exhibited at foundations across Europe.

«I WOULD LOVE TO MAKE PEOPLE DREAM ALL AROUND THE WORLD PRODUCING CREATIVITY AND STYLE.»

Matteo's distinctive process begins with color: he scours his favorite sources for millions of tiny pure silk threads, innately knowing which to weave together for his textiles to achieve a most unique and magical vibrancy. These threads are then cut at different lengths, uncovering different colors and exploding like fireworks and waterfalls all over to flatter the silhouette. His clothes dance in the way that they fit the body and follow its movements. The woman he designs for is both primal and sophisticated, unafraid to be herself or show her body.

ORSCHEL-READ
LONDON

Stéfan Orschel-Read won gold medals as a dressage rider for Great Britain and studied law prior to designing clothes. India-born and raised in Scotland, Stéfan realized early on that he could mix his broad array of tastes and talents with fashion design. He attended the prestigious Central Saint Martins receiving an Honors Degree in Menswear as well as completing a Masters at the Royal College of Art.

«FASHION TO ME IS LIKE PLAYING GOD, AND GREATLY HOPING SOMEONE MIGHT JUST PLAY ALONG.»

Stéfan finds inspiration in classic British literature; his collections have been themed after Virginia Woolf's 1928 novel *Orlando* and Shakespeare's *Twelfth Night*.

«THERE IS NO DIVIDE BETWEEN MEN AND WOMEN. THERE ARE DIFFERENCES BUT FAR MORE SIMILARITIES.» VIRGINIA WOOLF

But the references he makes with his clothing do not stop there: Hindu artwork and London's multicultural youth also figure heavily into this young designer's stimulating repertoire. His collections merge couture and Liberty prints with wearable silhouettes and accessible tailoring, marrying innovative leatherwork, contemporary pagan influences and organic materials.

«THERE IS TIME FOR WORK, AND TIME FOR LOVE. THAT LEAVES NO OTHER TIME.» COCO CHANEL

His pieces have been shot by the hippest photographers and featured in the most selective magazines. Fashion icons Lady Gaga and Naomi Campbell have worn several of his pieces. Stéfan's daring and evolved approach to life imbue all the fabrics he touches, turning them into sought-after treasures.

Stefán Orschel-Read *INTERVIEW*

___ WHAT WOULD YOU CONSIDER THE MOST DARING MO-
MENT IN FASHION HISTORY?

I believe that in the very near future we will experience an explosion
of creativity that will overshadow any from the past. Ours is the first
truly free generation. We are not constrained by set societal values, as
our parents were. In addition we are not motivated by rebellion. It is
in this era of freedom that the utmost creativity will be realized.

___ WHERE IS THE MOST UNIQUE OR SURPRISING PLACE
YOU HAVE BEEN INSPIRED FOR MATERIALS OR PATTERNS?

At a time when I was worried I was feeling uninspired, I found inspiration in an unlikely place. On a day trip to Stockholm I sat in the pews
of a church and looked up, and was fascinated by the ceiling murals of
the church. It is natural that at points one can become uninspired, but
one must have the confidence that inspiration will come often when
you do not expect it.

___ MANY DESIGNERS TODAY SAY THAT FASHION IS A KIND
OF STORYTELLING. IF SO, WHAT STORY WERE YOU TELL-
ING WITH YOUR LAST COLLECTION?

The inspiration for my bespoke collection 'Edges of the World,' showing in June 2011, comes from a children's storybook that I produced
and had bound, telling the story of a sailor in the fleet of Vasco da
Gama, in a quest to discover a new trade route to India in 1492.

right: Fall/Winter 2010

following pages:
"The Spy Who Becomes Me"
Spring/Summer 2011

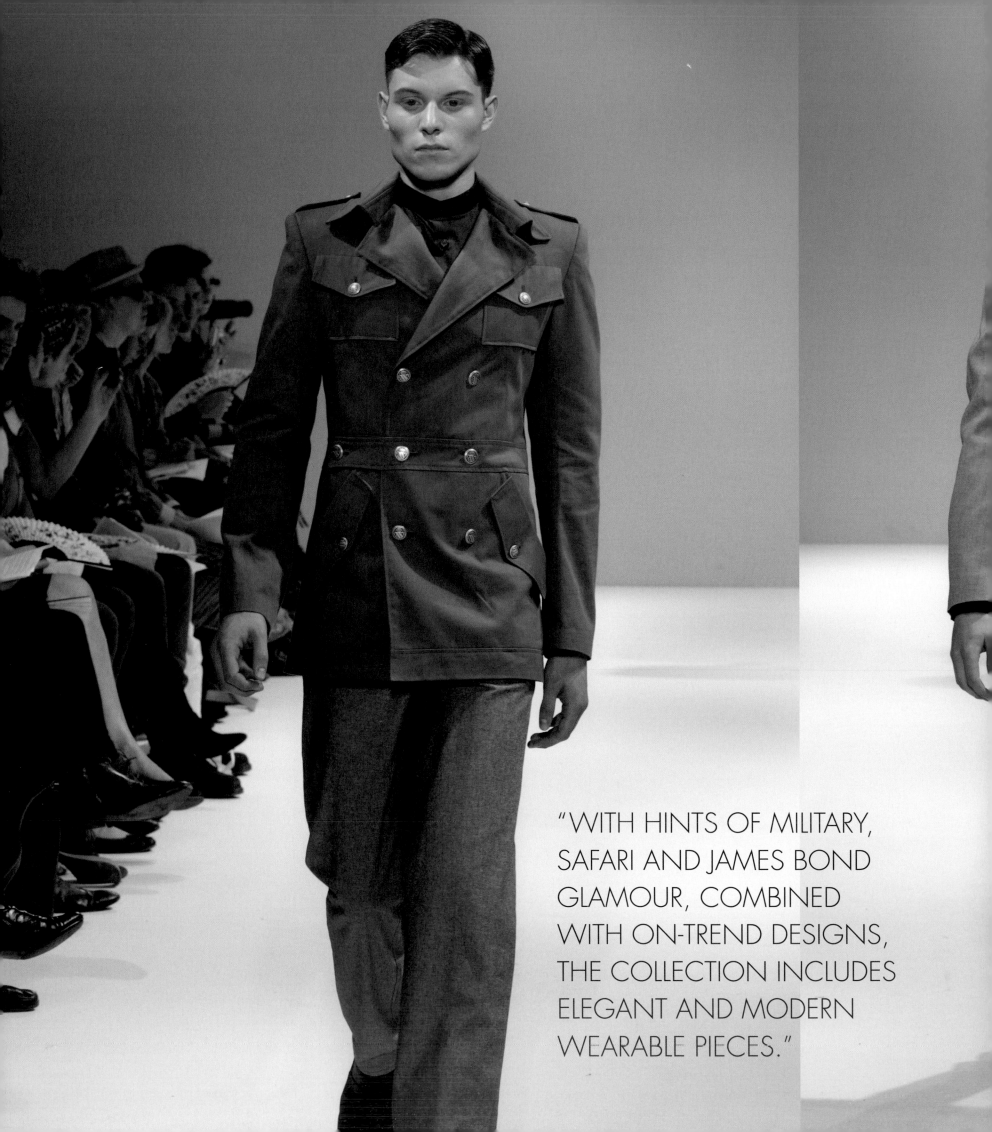

"WITH HINTS OF MILITARY, SAFARI AND JAMES BOND GLAMOUR, COMBINED WITH ON-TREND DESIGNS, THE COLLECTION INCLUDES ELEGANT AND MODERN WEARABLE PIECES."

PARKCHOONMOO
SEOUL

left and following pages:
Spring/Summer 2011

Demi (Choon-Moo) Park was born in Kimje, a small town in the southern part of Korea, where her family owned a children's apparel company. A happy fixture in her father's factory and showroom, Demi was fascinated by the transformative and reflective nature of clothing and hence her love of fashion was born. After her family moved to Seoul, Demi attended Hongik University, where she majored in industrial design, followed by the Kookje Fashion School where she studied fashion design.

«THIS COLLECTION IS HEAVILY REMINISCENT OF CHIC URBAN STREET WEAR. WITH MINIMAL USE OF COLOR—A PALETTE OF PRIMARILY GRAY AND BLACK—PARK-CHOONMOO LOOSELY DRAPED PIECES AND PAIRED THEM WITH CONSTRUCTED OVERCOATS AND SKINNY TIGHT BOTTOMS TO GIVE THEM A UNIQUE LOOK ALL THEIR OWN.» (ALEXANDRA DAWES FOR MODACYCLE.COM)

Her industrial design roots are evident in her fashion designs and have defined her compelling aesthetic. Having owned shops and worked in fashion since 1988, earning accolades and prestigious international awards along the way, Demi's designs have become iconic for their modern architecture and yet fluid style.

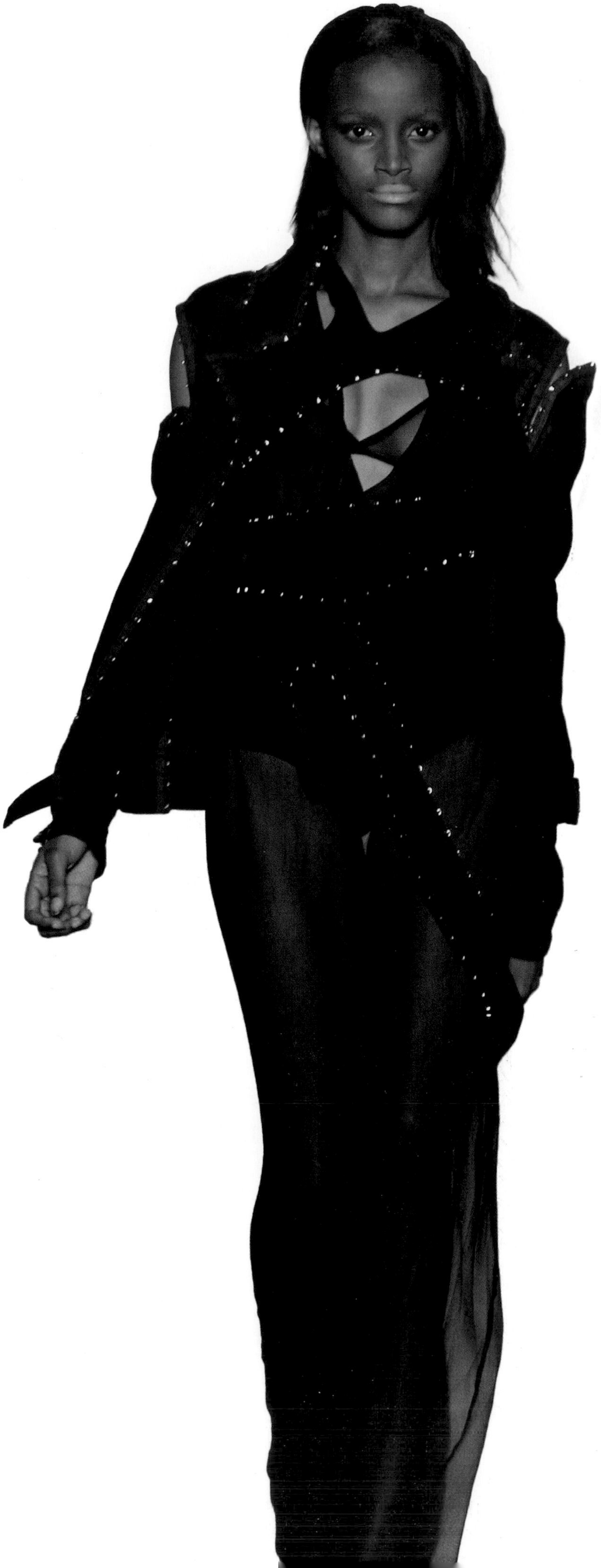

here and following pages:
Fall/Winter 2010

"GEOMETRIC SHAPES…
reveal dark layers of fabric in complementary textures"

"BEAUTIFUL BLACK
URBAN CHIC
MINIMALIST PALETTE
OF DARK STYLES AND
COLORS"

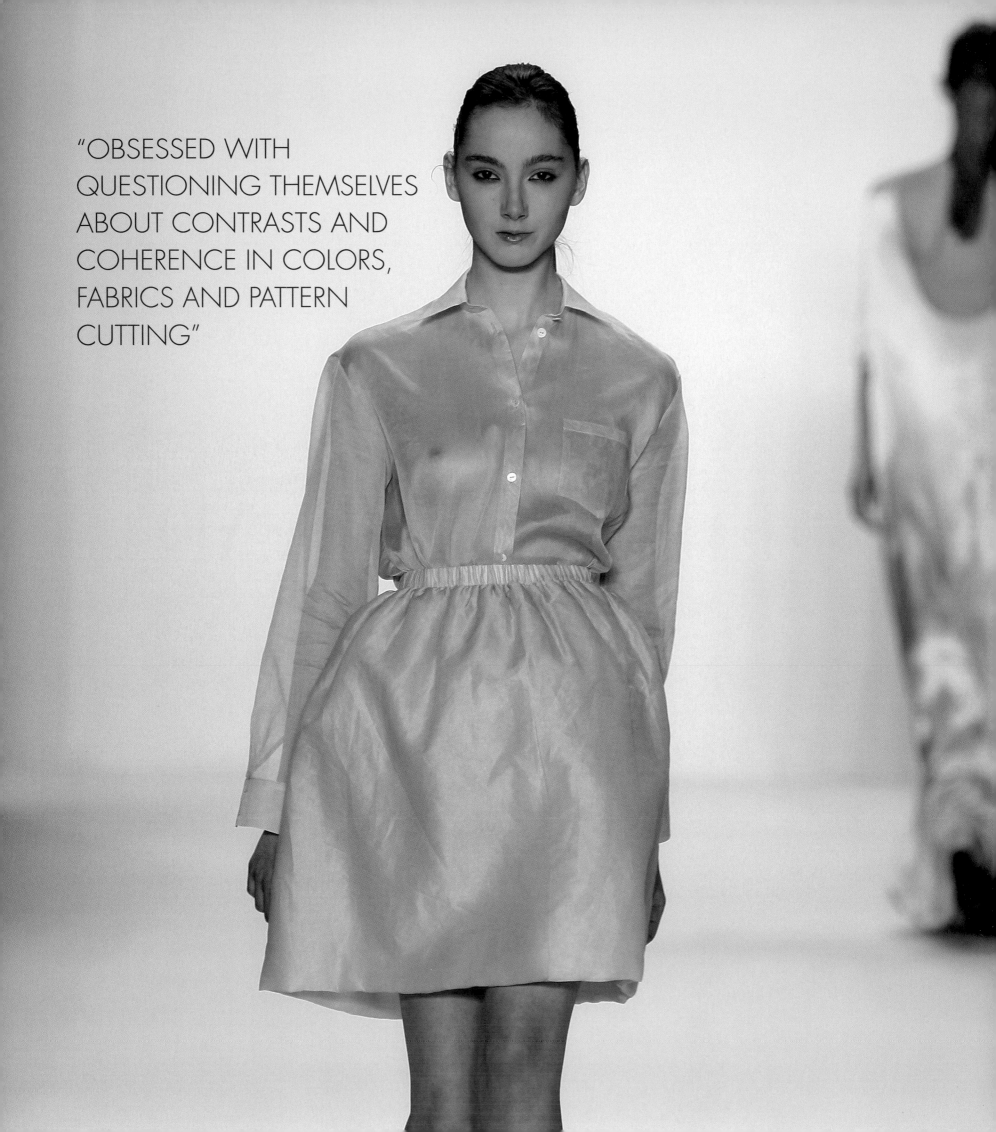

"OBSESSED WITH QUESTIONING THEMSELVES ABOUT CONTRASTS AND COHERENCE IN COLORS, FABRICS AND PATTERN CUTTING"

Johanna Perret and Tutia Schaad were nominated for several design awards for their work after graduating from Berlin Kunsthochschule Weißensee in 2009. Their talents led them both to the haute couture capital of Paris, where they worked in elite apprenticeships at Givenchy Haute-Couture and Prêt-à-Porter, Gaspard Yurkievich and Swash. Returning to Berlin from Paris to found their own label, which has drawn comparisons to Jil Sander, they participated at Who's Next and won a stipend from the Mercedes-Benz Fashion Week Berlin and the City of Berlin.

«PERRET SCHAAD CONTEMPLATES MODESTY WITH AMBITION. THEY REQUIRE THE FINEST QUALITY, FINDING IT IN INNOVATION AS WELL AS IN TRADITION.» (MERCEDES-BENZ FASHION WEEK BERLIN)

Their clothing sets a new paradigm for elegant simplicity. Though the clothing looks pure and eloquent, they have been made with the utmost care and technical complexity. The cuts having been questioned over and over again as though they were the riddle of the sphinx, producing in effect the most streamlined results.

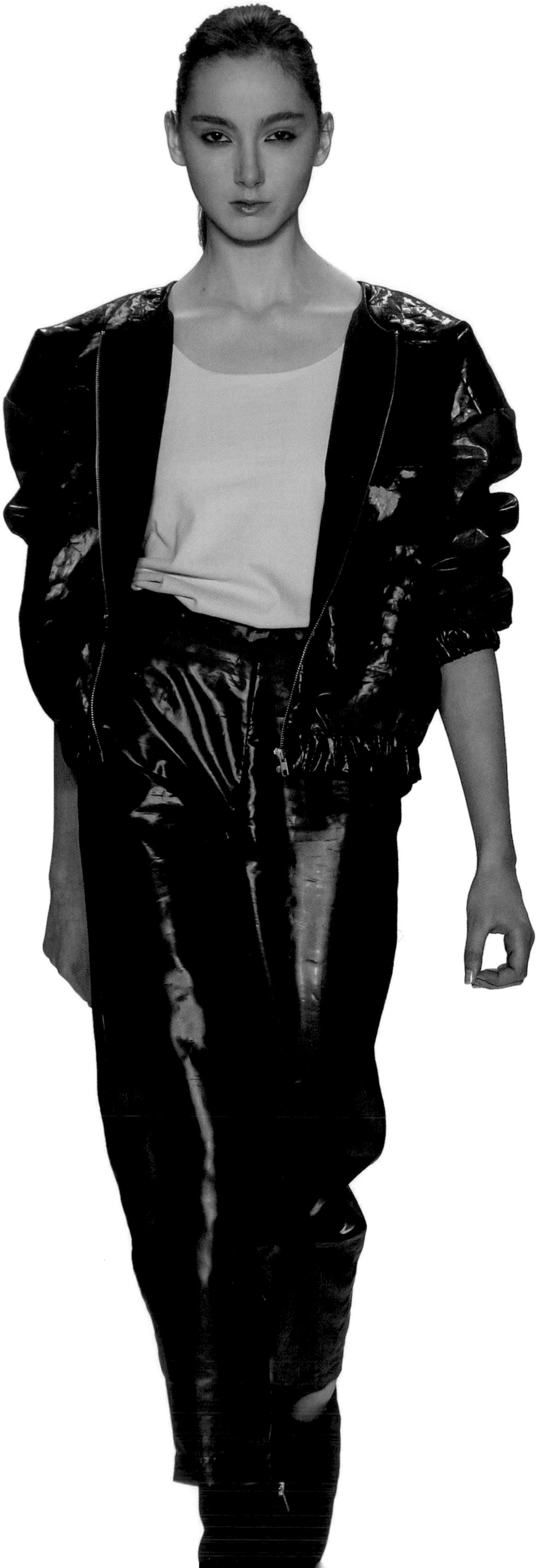

_____ *"SURPRISINGLY STRONG,*
accomplished tailoring"

"WITH A CLEAN, CLEAR VISION AND COMPARISONS TO JIL SANDER, THEY PROVE THERE IS HOPE FOR BERLIN FASHION AFTER ALL" (MONO-BLOG.COM)

RAD HOURANI
PARIS

Rad by Rad Hourani Collection #2
September 2010

following pages:
The largely monochromatic aesthetic boils over into
the studio's interior design

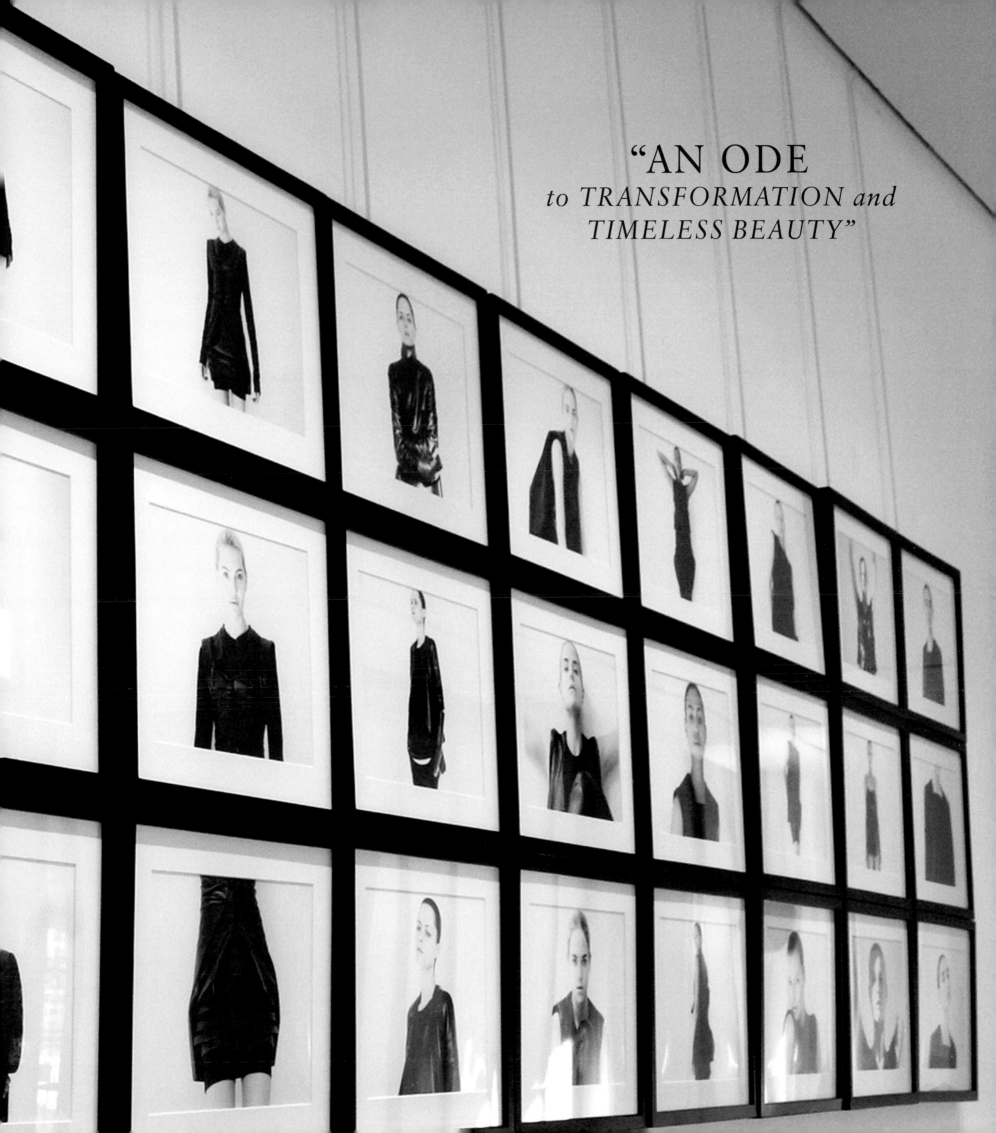

"AN ODE
to TRANSFORMATION *and*
TIMELESS BEAUTY"

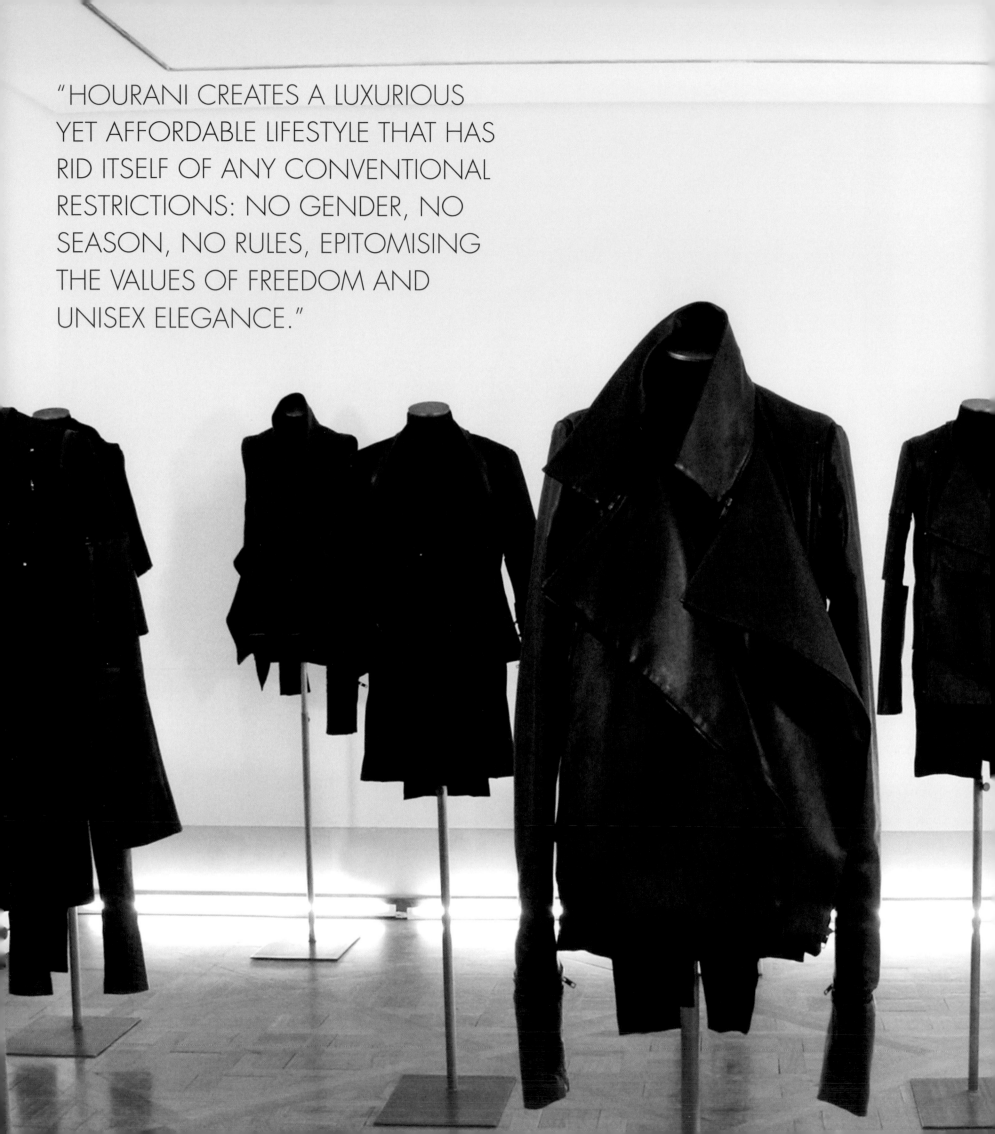

"HOURANI CREATES A LUXURIOUS YET AFFORDABLE LIFESTYLE THAT HAS RID ITSELF OF ANY CONVENTIONAL RESTRICTIONS: NO GENDER, NO SEASON, NO RULES, EPITOMISING THE VALUES OF FREEDOM AND UNISEX ELEGANCE."

Rad Hourani opted out of formal design education, preferring instead to earn his fashion pedigree from the school of hard knocks. This bad boy tendency is manifest in his errant, black designs. His adventures in Paris and other major cosmopolitan cities lend his clothes a modern European minimalist edge.

«I LIKE THE IDEA OF A WORLD THAT WE COULD LIVE AND SHAPE BY OURSELVES, ONLY BY OBSERVING. EACH OUR OWN. MY CLOTHES HAVE ERUPTED FROM THIS WORLD OF MINE. THEY ARE ASEXUAL, ASEASONAL, THEY COME FROM NO PLACE, NO TIME, NO TRADITION, YET THEY COULD BE HOME ANYWHERE, ANYTIME.»

Early on Rad was immersed in the fashion world as a model scout. He searched for unique beauty on the streets of Montreal, New York and Paris and also took jobs as a stylist. When he went on to set up his own line in Paris at the tender age of 25 he was already very well-versed in the fashion game.

«HOURANI DOES NOT CONSIDER HIMSELF TO BE EITHER A DESIGNER, NOR A PHOTOGRAPHER, NOR AN ARTIST, NOR A FILMMAKER, NOR A WRITER, NOR AN ART DIRECTOR, NOR AN ARCHITECT, NOR A MUSICIAN. HE IS ALL OF THAT IN ONE, WHICH GIVES HIM A WIDE SCOPE OF SELF EXPRESSION THAT PUTS HIS MARK ON EVERYTHING HE IS UNDERTAKING AND THAT NURTURES AND PUSHES FURTHER HIS VISION OF A WORLD WITHOUT ANY BOUNDARIES BE THEY PHYSICAL, MENTAL, OR GENDER-BASED.»

Driven by "curiosity and innocence," Rad dove head first into the world of fabrics and cuts. His "asexual, aseasonal" clothes are rife with androgynous appeal, making them *the* wardrobe for the coming apocalypse of sexiness.

left:
Black leather jackets in Hourani's studio

following pages:
Rad by Rad Hourani Collection #3
September 2010

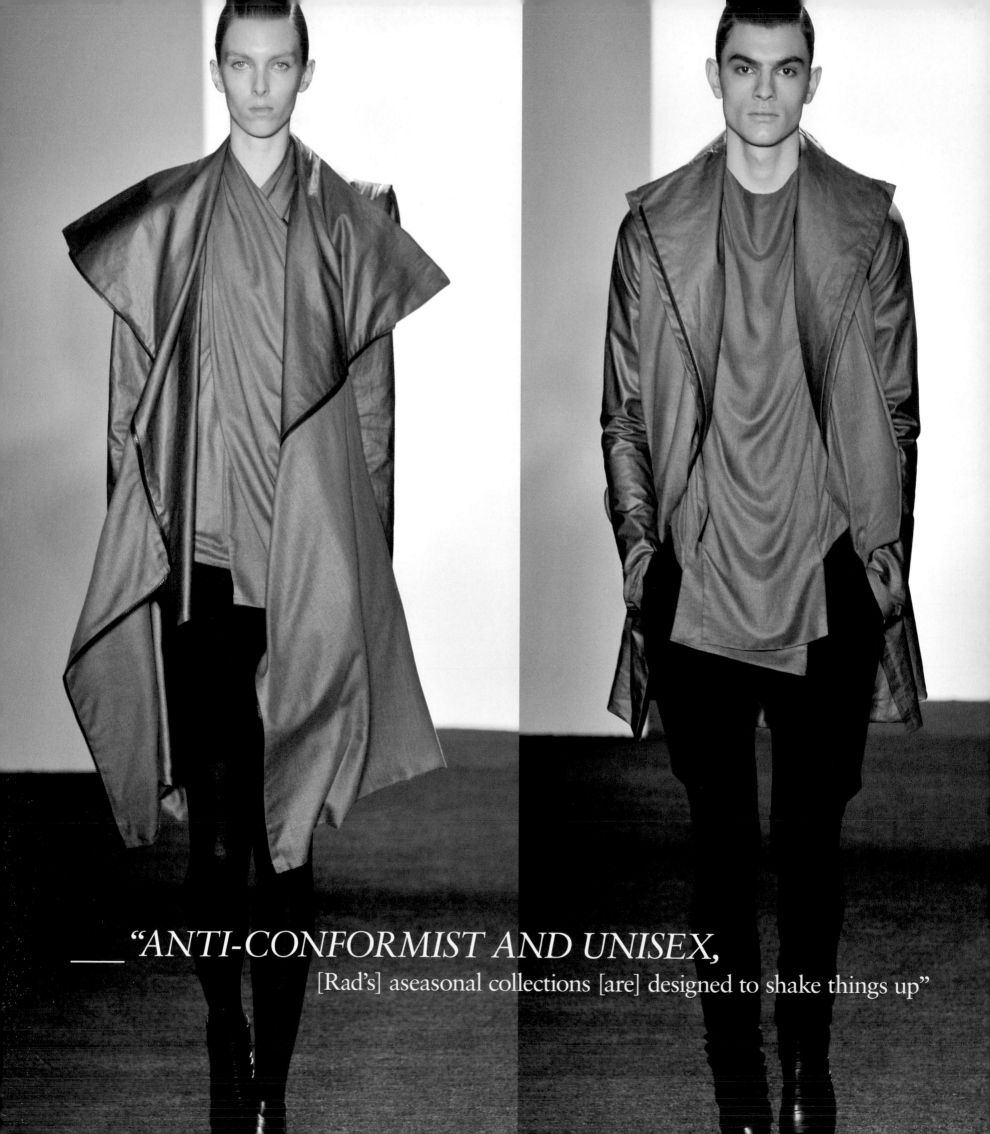

_ "ANTI-CONFORMIST AND UNISEX,
[Rad's] aseasonal collections [are] designed to shake things up"

"I STARTED IMAGINING CLOTHES
THE SAME WAY I STARTED CREATING
IMAGES: WITH A SENSE OF CURIOSITY
AND INNOCENCE DRIVEN BY MY NO-
BACKGROUND BACKGROUND. NO
SCHOOL. NO TEACHERS. NO TELLY.
NO BOUNDARIES. NO FORMATTING."

Rad by Rad Hourani Collection #2

following pages:
Rad by Rad Hourani Collection #6
September 2010

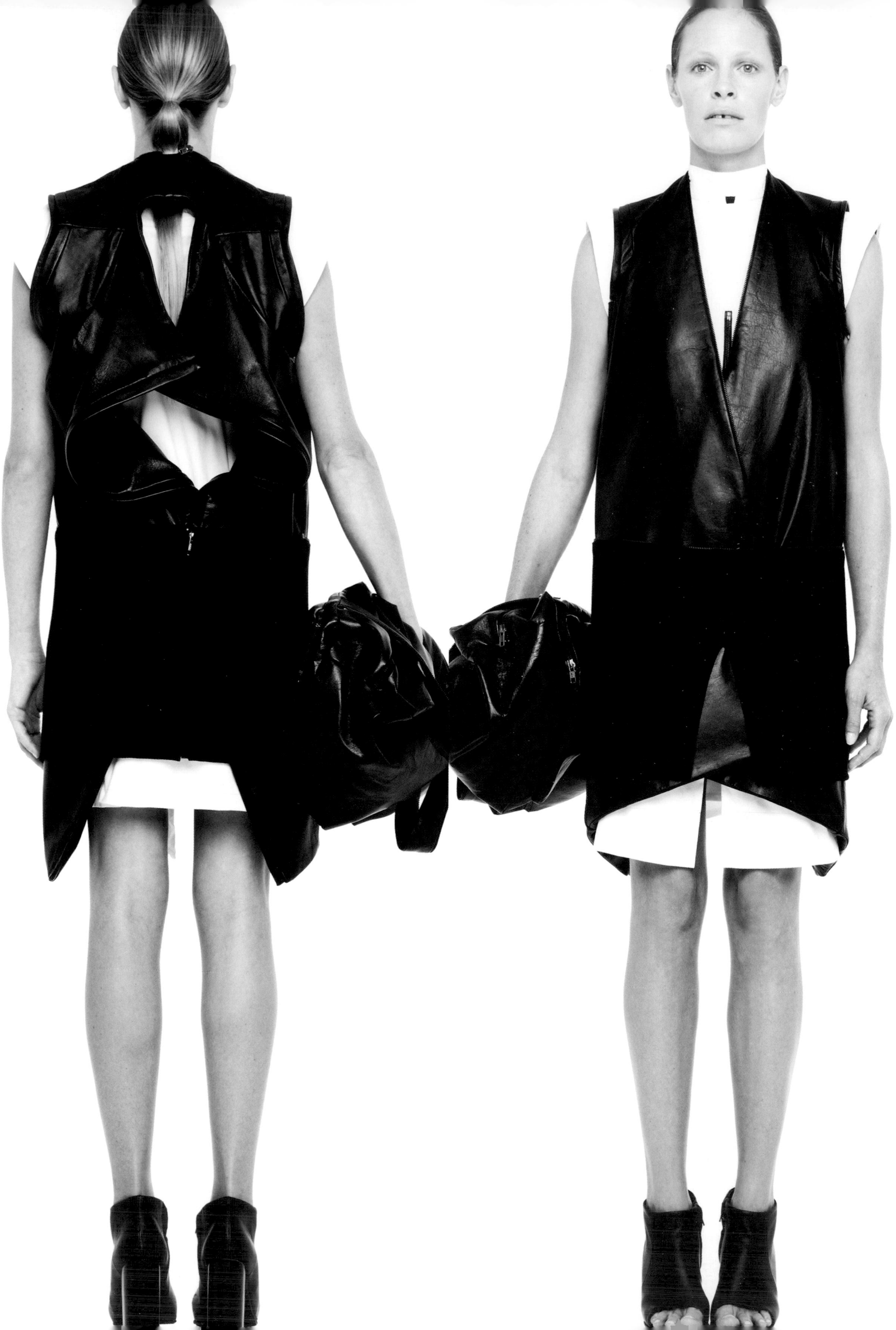

RISTO
PARIS

Risto has spent a life dedicated to worldly pursuits, much like his fellow Macedonian Alexander the Great. But rather than wielding force through violence, Risto's greatest strategy could be his use of sublime fabrics.

«I NEVER LOOK TO A MUSE.»

Born in 1974 and brought up in a socialist state, Risto found counter-culture solace in 80's MTV, the globally connective television network that served as Generation X's Facebook. His attachment to this satellite is perhaps what drove him out even further into the cosmos toward the allure of celestial bodies. His first collection exploded like a supernova, literally and figuratively, on the catwalk. His dresses, superimposed with eerie starscapes earned Risto a number of dedicated fans.

«I DO NOT IMAGINE WOMEN TO FIT MY CLOTHES BUT CLOTHES TO FIT WOMEN.»

His background has resulted in an exploration of the "East-West" balance, still very prominent in his collections to date. While maintaining a day job as the head knitwear designer at Louis Vuitton, Risto launched his own line, which can be described as "acid-chique." Towing the line between extreme beauty and danger, Risto draws on inspirations like celestial torrents and hawk's eyes.

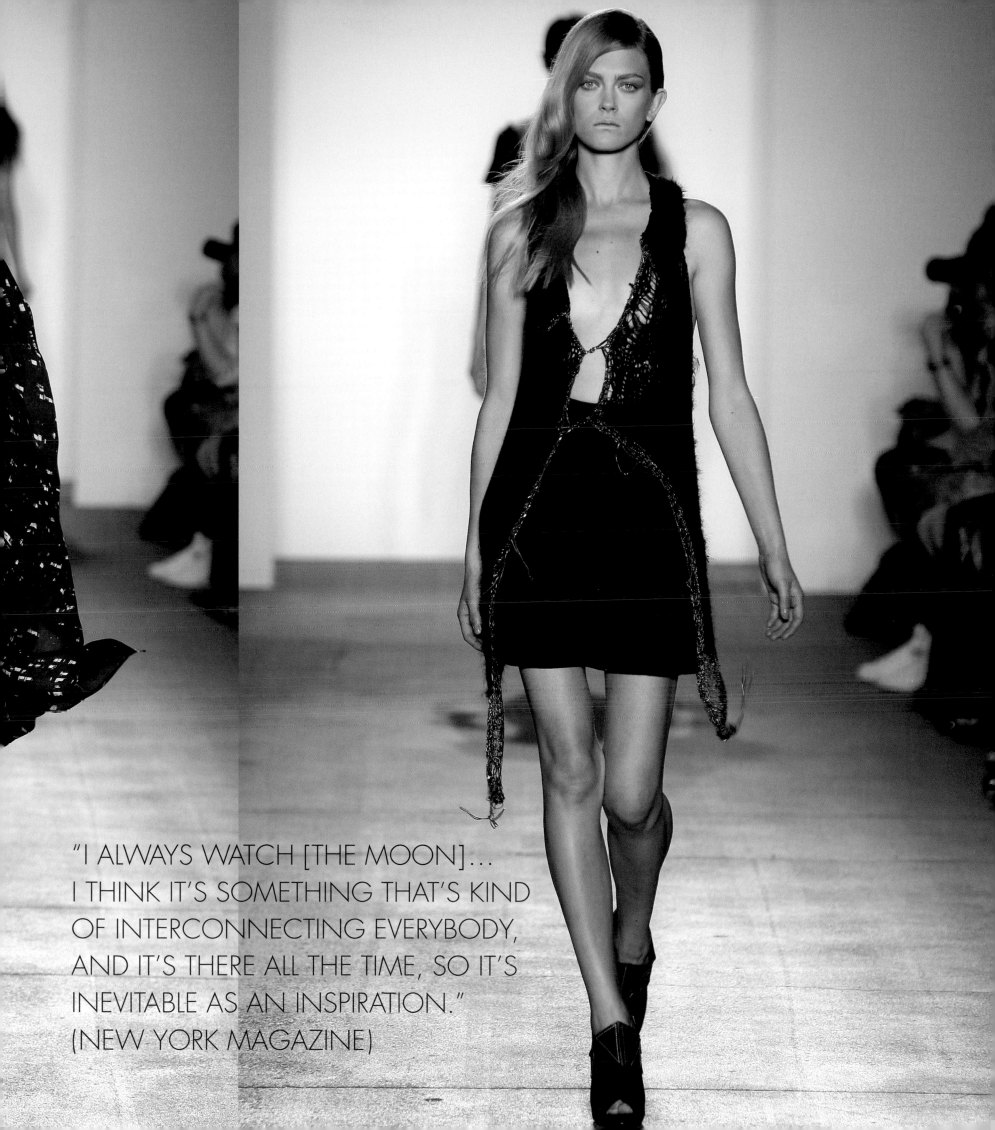

"I ALWAYS WATCH [THE MOON]…
I THINK IT'S SOMETHING THAT'S KIND
OF INTERCONNECTING EVERYBODY,
AND IT'S THERE ALL THE TIME, SO IT'S
INEVITABLE AS AN INSPIRATION."
(NEW YORK MAGAZINE)

Risto *INTERVIEW*

___ WHO DO YOU CONSIDER TO BE THE MOST STYLISH PERSON IN THE WHOLE WORLD?
Andy Warhol.
___ WHAT WILL YOU BE ADDING TO YOUR OWN WARDROBE THIS SPRING?
A straw hat.
___ WHAT IS YOUR FAVORITE PIECE OF CLOTHING OR ACCESSORY IN YOUR CLOSET?
A T-shirt from Maison Martin Margiela and my braided belt from Principe, Florence.
___ WHAT IS THE BEST LESSON YOU HAVE LEARNED ABOUT FASHION SINCE YOU STARTED YOUR COLLECTION?
Never launch all the ideas with the same supplier!
___ WHAT DESIGNER FROM THE PAST DO YOU THINK EXERTED THE MOST INFLUENCE ON FASHION TODAY?
Martin Margiela.
___ WHAT IS THE MOST UNIQUE OR SURPRISING PLACE YOU HAVE BEEN THAT INSPIRES MATERIALS OR PATTERNS?
The Archives of Mantero in Como, Italy.
___ WHAT IS ONE OF YOUR FAVORITE FASHION TRENDS FROM THE PAST?
Casting Sauvage.

right and following pages:
Fall/Winter 2010

___ "GRUNGE DETAILS
inspired by high school and pixelated digital art"

RONALD
ABDALA
BEIRUT

"In Bloom" collection
Fall/Winter 2010

"EDGY YET FEMININE COLLECTIONS TARGET FASHION FORWARD WOMEN THAT DON'T SHY AWAY FROM EDGY SILHOUETTES."

"MY MAIN FOCUS IS BALANCE;
balancing out European style with the Mediterranean allure"

left:
*The Marlene dress from the
"Cinema" collection*
Fall/Winter 2009

following pages:
The *Athena dress
from the "Divinity" collection*
Spring/Summer 2009

Ronald Abdala *INTERVIEW*

___ WHEN DID YOU FIRST BECOME INTERESTED IN FASHION?
It was during the 90's era of Madonna's "Vogue" and Deee-lite's "Groove is in the Heart." I've been drawing ever since my childhood, but that was the period that sparked my interest in fashion.
___ WHAT IS MORE IMPORTANT: CLOTHE THE FEMALE BODY IN AN ARTISTIC WAY, OR SENSUALIZE THE FEMALE?
For me it's about sensualizing the female body. But one doesn't have to exclude the other. You can sensualize the female form in an artistic way.
___ WHAT IS YOUR FAVORITE PIECE OF CLOTHING OR ACCESSORY IN YOUR CLOSET?
My black, brown and grey clown Bottega Veneta shoes.

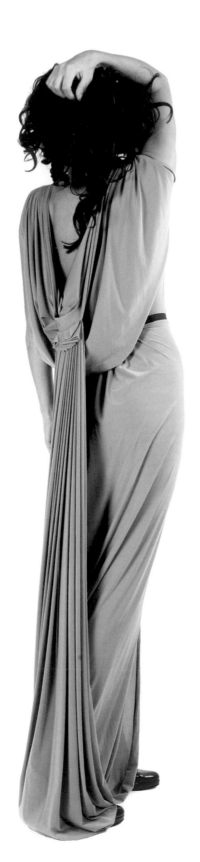

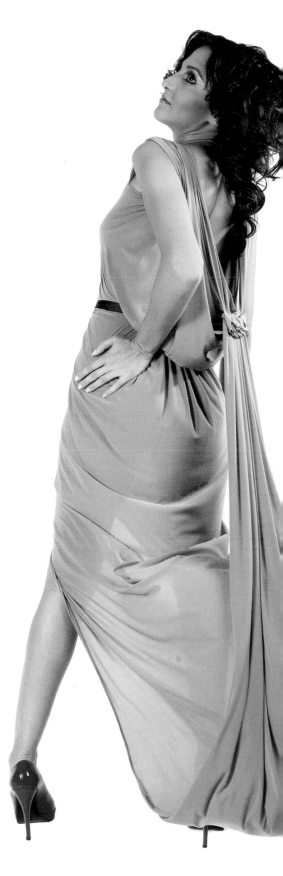

SIKI IM
NEW YORK

right and following pages:
Spring/Summer 2011

Siki Im's strong menswear line is perfectly suited to the urban landscape of New York City where the designer's creativity thrives. His aesthetic pays attention to the toughness that can be found on the flipside of beauty. Prior to fashion, Siki received top honors from Oxford College of Architecture and worked on many projects throughout the world, so it's no wonder that when he turned his attention to fabric, he decided to emphasize structure.

«THERE ARE TOO MANY QUOTES AND MOTTOS TO LIVE BY. [I THINK THE MOST IMPORTANT THING IS] JUST BE HONEST AND TRY NOT TO JUDGE.»

There's a palpable "brick-and-mortar" stability in his clothing that doesn't just come from hardy fabrics and careful construction. Siki's clothes look like they have survival instincts. A recent collection entitled "The Island" symbolizes a new era of *Lord of the Flies*.

«HOPEFULLY MY COLLECTION PORTRAYS A FEELING OR EMOTION. IT DOESN'T MATTER IF IT'S GOOD OR BAD.»

The essence of this, and all of Siki's collections to date, is that resourcefulness, power and durability must draw on an eclectic range of ethnic and subcultural influences to remain progressive and wearable.

SIKI IM *INTERVIEW*

___ IF YOU COULD DESIGN ANYTHING ELSE OTHER THAN FASHION, WHAT WOULD IT BE?
A church. A yacht.
___ WHO DO YOU CONSIDER TO BE THE MOST STYLISH PERSON IN THE WHOLE WORLD?
Homeless people.
___ WHERE IS THE MOST UNIQUE OR SURPRISING PLACE YOU HAVE BEEN INSPIRED FOR MATERIALS OR PATTERNS?
Iran.
___ WHAT IS MORE IMPORTANT: TO CLOTHE THE FEMALE BODY IN AN ARTISTIC WAY, OR SENSUALIZE THE FEMALE?
Both go hand in hand. It can't be one or the other.
___ WHICH THREE ADJECTIVES DESCRIBE YOUR COLLECTION AND FASHION PHILOSOPHY?
Quiet. Strong. Minimal.
___ WHAT FACTORS DO YOU FEEL PARTICULARLY AFFECT YOUNG FASHION DESIGNERS TODAY?
Impatience. Social media. Minimums of quantities.
___ MANY DESIGNERS TODAY SAY THAT FASHION IS A KIND OF STORYTELLING. IF SO, WHAT STORY WERE YOU TELLING WITH YOUR LAST COLLECTION?
It has been a very personal and spiritual walk I have been experiencing, especially throughout the design process.
___ WHAT PERSONALITY TRAITS DO YOU THINK EVERY FASHION DESIGNER HAS TO HAVE TO START OUT IN THIS BUSINESS?
Patience. Rigorousness. Balance.
___ WHAT IS THE BEST EXPERIENCE YOU CAN SHARE ABOUT YOUR VERY FIRST CATWALK SHOW?
That my close loved ones were watching, especially my mother.
WHAT OR WHO INSPIRES YOU?
Indigenous cultures. New York City. My girlfriend.

right and following pages:
Fall/Winter 2010

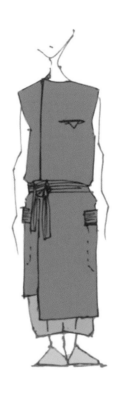

___ "DARK AND WOOLY FABRICS,
there is something uniquely comforting and protective about them"

SILVIO BETTERELLI

MILAN

"Umbras" collection
Spring/Summer 2011

Silvio Betterelli left the idyllic island of Sardinia to pursue his lifelong passion of design in the fast-paced urban cityscape of Milan. Thank god for the ease of 21st travel—if he hadn't made it to the continent, fashionistas would be enacting a Viking-style invasion as we speak. Once on the mainland, Silvio received degrees in Art of Fabric, Fashion Design, Fine Art and Textile Design from an array of schools located around Europe and the globe, broadening his knowledge of different tastes and techniques.

«I'M VERY INTERESTED IN DESIGN, ART AND ARCHITECTURE, I BUY MORE PRODUCT DESIGN MAGAZINES THAN FASHION MAGAZINES, AND I ALWAYS PAY ATTENTION TO WHAT I EXPERIENCE EVERYDAY, THE SIMPLE THINGS IN PARTICULAR. THE BEGINNING OF MY NEXT COLLECTION COULD BE HIDDEN EVEN IN THE MORNING COFFEE CUP.»

His intelligent masterpieces are therefore a mix of old and new, of traditional, classically Sardinian artistry and styles culled from around the world. He has introduced the ancient practice of Apulian embroidery to the urbanite living thousands of miles away, keeping the heritage of his unique island with its pink sand beaches home very much alive.

«I THINK IT IS SOME KIND OF CONTRADICTION IN FASHION TO HAVE STRICT FIXED REFERENCES, BECAUSE EVERY SEASON EVERYTHING RENEWS, EVERYTHING CHANGES.»

In addition to believing that classical techniques are universally inspiring, Silvio believes that good design can lead to a wider overall consciousness of the world around us, which is why he is an active participant in the experimental design collective S.M.o.g. Silvio's work links history and forgotten craftsmanship to contemporary design, producing clothes that are mystical and modern.

Silvio Betterelli *INTERVIEW*

___ WHAT IS YOUR FAVORITE PIECE OF CLOTHING TO WORK WITH?

I love to work on sheath dresses—a small but continuous challenge. They are all very plain and feminine. I have to create every time something special without going out of the silhouette and with the bond of the proportion lines of the sheath dress.

___ IF YOU COULD DESIGN ANYTHING ELSE OTHER THAN FASHION, WHAT WOULD IT BE?

Basically, I'm already doing that, because I design objects for home with a group of friends. We are called "smogmilano." It's very fun, and we also have a moderate interest from the press and insiders thanks to our ironic approach. Creating a chair, cutlery or a plate, or spending the day at the glass blower, which produces the glasses that I designed, is truly inspiring. This multidisciplinary approach is essential in order to carry on my work as a fashion designer. I often betray fashion and I do it very willingly.

___ HOW DO YOU FEEL ABOUT EXPERIMENTAL FASHION AS ART AS COMPARED TO FASHION NECESSARY TO PRODUCE FOR COMMERCIAL SUCCESS?

It's a continuous conflict. When you work on a collection you always try to do your best and not restrict yourself about research and experimentation. I create pieces that will hardly sell, and I know that when I design them; but at the same time I try to distill from my research pieces that have a more commercial sense. At the end of the selling campaign we realize that what we sell the most are the special pieces, and the price or the wearability are not so important. Fashion is a segment of product design. The fact that nowadays in product design there is a more deep interest in "art-design" and in unique pieces, is a very important signal that will involve fashion more and more, for sure.

___ WHERE IS THE MOST UNIQUE OR SURPRISING PLACE YOU HAVE BEEN INSPIRED FOR MATERIALS OR PATTERNS?

I travel a lot and I look very carefully at everything around me. This has allowed me a contemporary look at my land, Sardinia, which is full of suggestions.

___ WHO (OR WHAT) INSPIRES YOU?

Everything that happens everyday, but surfaces in particular: what I see, touch, live in every moment of the day.

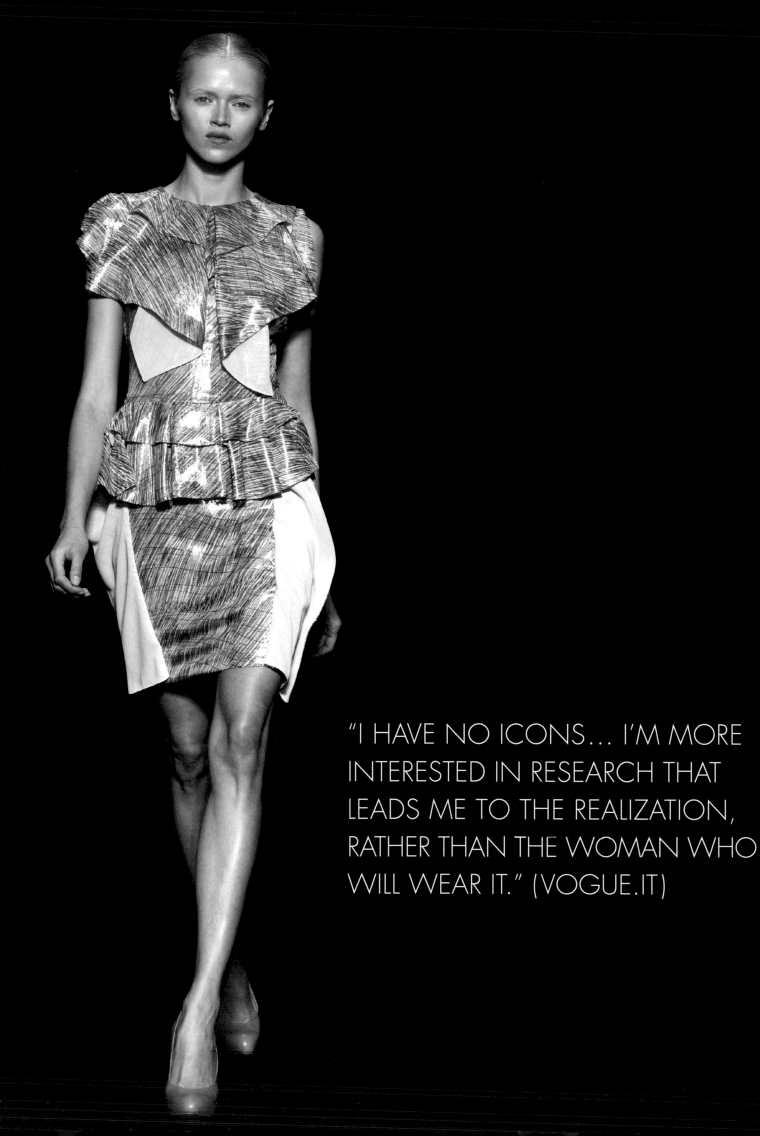

"I HAVE NO ICONS… I'M MORE INTERESTED IN RESEARCH THAT LEADS ME TO THE REALIZATION, RATHER THAN THE WOMAN WHO WILL WEAR IT." (VOGUE.IT)

"[I AM INSPIRED BY] EVERYTHING THAT HAPPENS EVERYDAY, BUT SURFACES IN PARTICULAR: WHAT I SEE, TOUCH, LIVE IN EVERY MOMENT OF THE DAY."

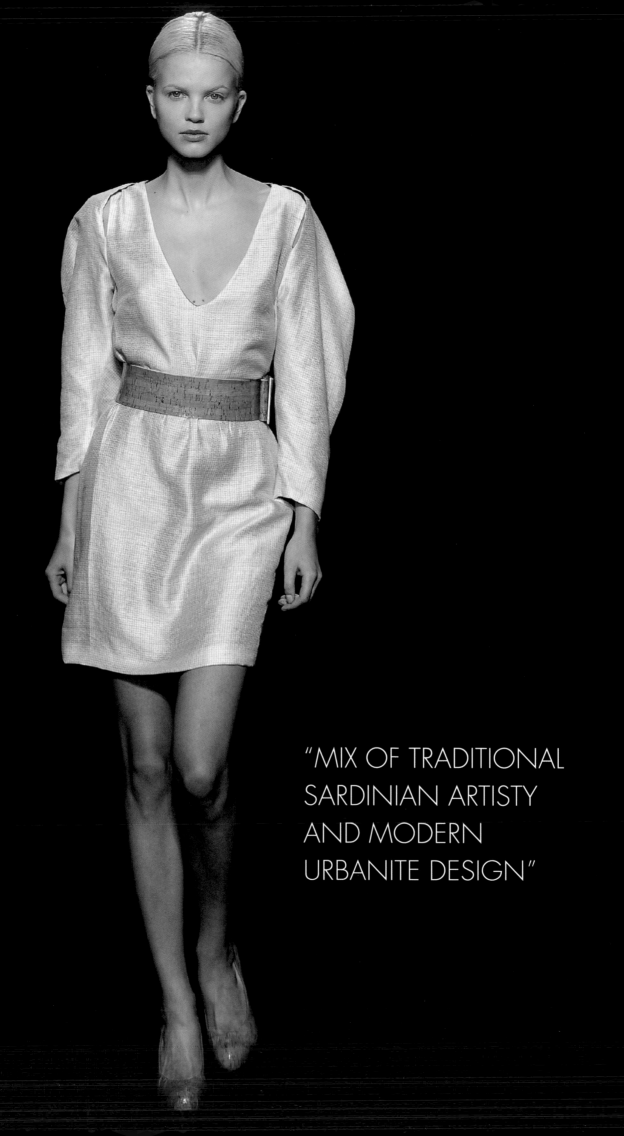

"MIX OF TRADITIONAL
SARDINIAN ARTISTY
AND MODERN
URBANITE DESIGN"

STEFFIE CHRISTIAENS

PARIS

*The intense blues in this collection symbolize the
color of the most heated part of flames and fire*
Fall/Winter 2011

Steffie Christiaens completed fashion design studies at the IFM in Paris and the Arnhem Academy in the Netherlands. Upon graduating from IFM in 2009, Steffie was selected as a finalist in the prestigious Hyères Festival in the south of France. From there she went on to work in the ateliers of Balenciaga and the Maison Martin Margiela between 2007 and 2010 until she finally established her own studio in Paris in 2010.

«A COUTURIER MUST BE AN ARCHITECT FOR DESIGN, A SCULPTOR FOR SHAPE, A PAINTER FOR COLOR, A MUSICIAN FOR HARMONY, AND A PHILOSOPHER FOR TEMPERANCE.» CRISTOBAL BALENCIAGA

Steffie pursues a conceptual design process through womens and mens ready-to-wear collections, utilizing her knowledge and training in the fields of fabric design, 3-D construction and printing. She imbues a deep personal ideology and an abstract mythology into her garments. Constantly challenging traditional garment codes through her experimentation with elemental forces and the asymmetry of nature, Steffie Christiaens provokes a new dialogue in the converging realms of art and fashion.

Both the colors and the beautifully warped structures in this collection were inspired by the science of heat
Fall/Winter 2011

__"CONSTANTLY CHALLENGING

traditional garment codes"

Steffie Christiaens *INTERVIEW*

__ WHAT IS THE ONE SENTENCE THAT DESCRIBES WHAT FASHION MEANS TO YOU?
A journey to find something new, an eternal search that is never fulfilled.

__ IF YOU COULD DESIGN ANYTHING ELSE OTHER THAN FASHION, WHAT WOULD IT BE?
I would like to design a building to explore shapes and design in relation to the wider space around the human form.

__ HOW DO YOU FEEL ABOUT EXPERIMENTAL FASHION AS ART AS COMPARED TO THE FASHION NECESSARY TO PRODUCE FOR COMMERCIAL SUCCESS?
It's natural that I feel more excited to work on experimental pieces, but I also like to challenge the commercial possibilities. I like to make people recognize something experimental in the simplest of things.

__ WHAT IS YOUR OVERALL APPROACH TO DESIGN?
I always start with a concept, with a process that starts most of the time with research using vintage garments combined with an energy source that has the power to change them in different ways, such as wind, water or heat. By re-imagining these archetypes of clothing with this force, I capture the coincidence by taking pictures. Those pictures are my starting point to work on new silhouettes, lines and fabric directions.

__ WHAT ARE YOUR FUTURE GOALS IN FASHION?
To build a strong and thriving business so that I can continue to realize interesting projects and collections without restrictions and to be self-sufficient.

__ WHERE IS THE MOST UNIQUE OR SURPRISING PLACE YOU HAVE BEEN INSPIRED FOR MATERIALS OR PATTERNS?
I was hugely influenced by an abandoned industrial island I visited in St. Petersburg, Russia. There was an amazing energy, with all sorts of strange creative, passionate people engaged in all manner of unexpected activities. There were dramatic contrasts of isolation and togetherness, an ebb and flow of energy.

__ WHAT KIND OF WOMAN/MAN DO YOU DESIGN FOR THE MOST?
I design for people who are independent and can interpret their own style through each piece—not an army of clones. They are artistic and strong.

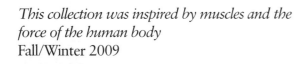

TÔ LONG-NAM

PARIS

*This collection was inspired by muscles and the
force of the human body*
Fall/Winter 2009

TÔ Long-Nam took up the sewing needle just seconds after mastering control of his motor-skills, which is to say he was very young when he began. But he desired more than to be a self-taught prodigy, so he attended Fashion Design school at the Academy of Fine Arts Berlin-Weissensee/Germany before moving to Paris where he worked with internationally renowned top-class stylists and for LANVIN menswear.

«A LOT OF THINGS LOOK ALIKE, BUT THEY'RE NOT NECESSARILY VERY MUCH ALIKE.» DONALD JUDD

His immaculate creations were recognized by the fashion powers in the industry and he was nominated for Hyères' 21st International Fashion and Photography Festival in short order. He showed his first collection here, and it was the deafening amount of positive feedback that incited him to launch his own label.

«OVER THE YEARS I HAVE LEARNED THAT WHAT IS IMPORTANT IN A DRESS IS THE WOMAN WHO IS WEARING IT.» YVES SAINT LAURENT

And the intensity with which he took to that measuring tape and those push-pins so early in life shows in the typically masculine, tailored-edge that defines his award winning fabrications. The TÔ Long-Nam woman looks sharp and sexy in architecturally sound yet fluid constructions.

This collection was inspired by the tuxedo
Spring/Summer 2010

TÔ Long-Nam *INTERVIEW*

__ WHAT IS THE BEST LESSON YOU HAVE LEARNED ABOUT
FASHION SINCE YOU STARTED YOUR COLLECTION?
Fashion is like everything else. Nowadays, first and foremost, it is after
all a business.
__ IF YOU COULD DRESS ONE CELEBRITY, WHO WOULD
IT BE?
Monica Vitti.
__ WHO IS A MAJOR STYLE ICON IN YOUR EYES?
Kate Moss.
__ WHAT IS YOUR FAVORITE COLOR AND WHY?
I agree with Coco Chanel who once said that the best color in the
whole world is the one that looks good on you.

right and following pages:
Fall/Winter 2009

"WOMEN WHO ARE AWARE OF THEIR QUALITIES BY JUST BEING THEMSELVES ARE THE WORLD'S MOST BEAUTIFUL CREATURES."

YOTAM SOLOMON
LOS ANGELES

Yotam Solomon approaches fashion in the same way he once approached fine art school or the viola: with the dynamic talent of a virtuso.

«[FASHION] IS ABOUT THINKING OUTSIDE OF THE BOX, AND WORKING TO IMPROVE EVERY SINGLE ASPECT OF FASHION ITSELF.»

The refinement of one of Yotam's dresses, with its powerful sense of self-expression, has all the makings of an orchestral masterpiece: the delicate beauty of the violin, the fluidity of the harp, the energy of the organ. He conducts his sartorial arrangements from a breezy studio in Los Angeles that has been his home since moving from Israel while in high school.

«WE DON'T JUST MAKE FASHION; WE CREATE IT FROM SO MANY DIFFERENT ELEMENTS AS IT HAS TO BE MEANINGFUL.»

Attending Beverly Hills High School, Yotam soaked up California youth-culture and a great casual-chic style to blend with the high classicism ideals of the aesthetic values with which he was raised. In addition to his relationship with fine art, Yotam finds inspiration and solace in nature. In honor of its fragile beauty, he recently designed a collection to raise awareness and funds for the victims of the BP Oil Spill in the Gulf of Mexico, proving that Yotam is a designer of both consummate taste and admirable awareness.

Yotam Solomon *INTERVIEW*

___ IF YOU COULD DESIGN ANYTHING ELSE OTHER THAN FASHION, WHAT WOULD IT BE?

If I could design anything else other than fashion it would be architectural structures. I recently renovated my home on Sunset Strip in Los Angeles. I literally took it apart and added levels which was a great deal of fun especially during the sketching and engineering period. I am also interested in designing interior products, hardware and automobiles in the future.

___ WHAT DOES THE NAME OF YOUR LABEL SIGNIFY?

My name is symbolic since it has different meanings. In the Old Testament of the Bible there is a story about Yotam who was the son of a famous Judge. As the story tells, Yotam was first and foremost a survivor; secondly, he had an incredible experience with nature and was also the youngest in his family. I can relate to all of those objectives and was certain it would be wise to have the line eponymous.

___ WHAT IS MORE IMPORTANT: TO CLOTHE THE FEMALE BODY IN AN ARTISTIC WAY, OR SENSUALIZE THE FEMALE?

It's all about empowering the wearer. Female or male fashion is about style which must consist of comfort, individualism and construction. These are the key factors.

___ IF YOU COULD DRESS ONE CELEBRITY, WHO WOULD IT BE?

I was lucky enough to already work with one of my inspirations Mrs. Victoria Beckham, who is an amazing individual and truly an icon.

___ WHAT IS THE BEST LESSON YOU HAVE LEARNED ABOUT FASHION SINCE YOU STARTED YOUR COLLECTION?

It's about having it all: style, design innovation, business savvy, great supporters and friends. You need everything and more to become successful in fashion.

___ HOW DO YOU FEEL ABOUT EXPERIMENTAL FASHION AS ART AS COMPARED TO THE FASHION NECESSARY TO PRODUCE FOR COMMERCIAL SUCCESS?

This is one of my favorite subjects as I design avant-garde fashion and live in Los Angeles. There is a lack of understanding about this issue. Fashion can be endlessly majestic, as haute fashion designers have a need to create wearable art where there is an idea behind a collection. A fashion piece can have the most divine construction and be made with exquisite materials, yet if it doesn't symbolize anything it loses its purpose. It's truly my goal in life to empower others and share innovation through my collections. For Spring 2011 I had the privilege to design a collection inspired by the BP Oil Spill; the response was phenomenal, showing the people do want more than just wear a piece of clothing. For Fall 2011 I decided to venture into a more infamous subject exploring the connection between Drugs and our DNA; along with modern living and educating others about this important issue. I hope to share and empower others with each collection as it's truly about the message, and not less importantly sustainable ethics and great construction.

"FASHION CAN BE ENDLESSLY MAJESTIC, AS HAUTE FASHION DESIGNERS HAVE A NEED TO CREATE WEARABLE ART WHERE THERE IS AN IDEA BEHIND A COLLECTION. A FASHION PIECE CAN HAVE THE MOST DIVINE CONSTRUCTION AND MADE WITH EXQUISITE MATERIALS, YET IF IT DOESN'T SYMBOLIZE ANYTHING IT LOSES ITS PURPOSE."

Spring/Summer 2010

YOUNG LILEE
LONDON

Young Lilee was one of two graduating students awarded a special distinction after presenting her very first line at the London College of Fashion's Masters Degree fashion show in 2010. Her exquisite structural ribbon-embellished dresses took notice from both a tough academic panel and seasoned buyers.

«SOUTH KOREAN DESIGNER YOUNG LILEE ASSERTS A PLAYFUL AND PHILOSOPHICAL IDENTITY.»

The large luxury department store Selfridge's won the race for Young, scooping her up to design a special line of bespoke collections when she was just fresh right out of school. While always defined by excellent tailoring, Young's designs explore various kinds of femininity and beauty, from the traditional (crisp white dresses) to the more unconventional (black Gothic veils). The uber-dexterous Young has earned plenty of blue ribbon prestige for her unique line of dresses.

"SNAKING ITS WAY AROUND THE GARMENT, THE BROCADE IS USED TO GREAT EFFECT, DEFINING THE CURVES OF THE BODY." (MARIECLAIRE.CO.UK)

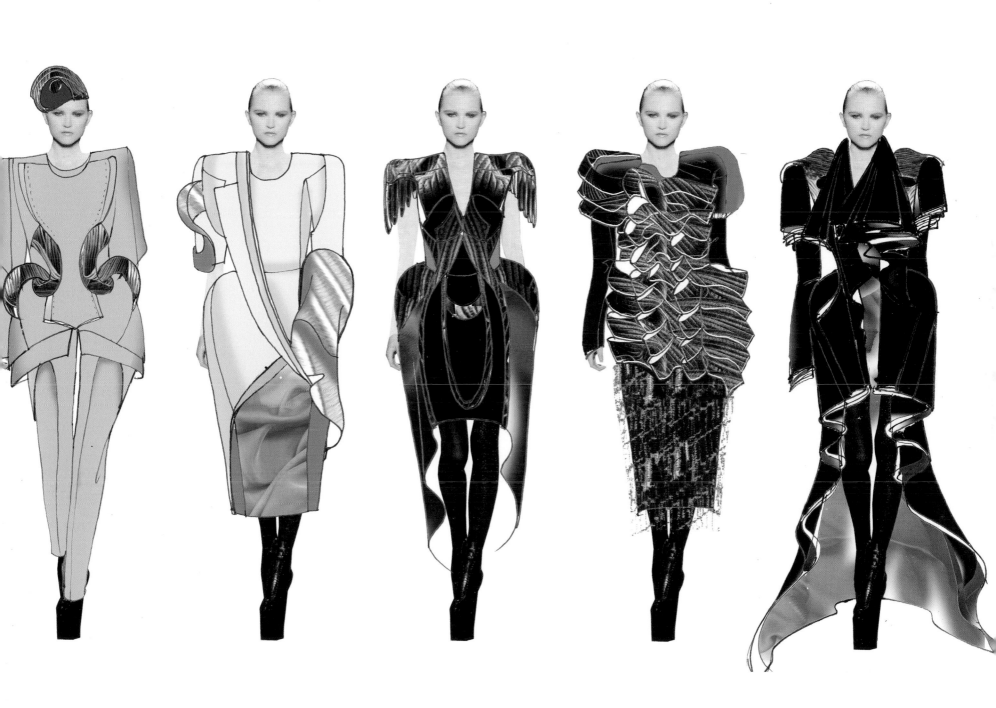

"MY COLLECTIONS [ARE] INSPIRED BY THE STRENGTH OF WOMEN."

Fall/Winter 2010

following pages:
Spring/Summer 2011

APPLAUSE

Introduction
© Patrick McMullan Company (p 11)
© Jonathan Grassi (p 12)

Ada Zanditon
© Paul Persky (pp 14–19)
www.adaz.co.uk

Alice Palmer
© Christopher Dadey (pp 20–29)
www.alicepalmer.co.uk

Bec & Bridge
© Harold David (pp 30–37)
www.becandbridge.com.au

Christian Cota
© Kevin Sturman (pp 40–47)
www.christiancota.com

Cushnie & Ochs
© Thomas Kletecka (pp 48–57)
© Huge Lippe (pp 58–59)
www.cushnieetochs.com

Delia Covezzi
© Delia Covezzi (pp 60–69)
www.deliacovezzi.com

Dora Mojzes
© Tamas Dobos (pp 70, 73)
© Mark Viszlay (pp 72, 74–77)
www.doramojzes.com

Edward Finney
© Anthony Sajdler (pp 78–87)
www.edwardfinney.com

Elisa Palomino
© Martin Scott Powell (pp 88–99)
www. elisapalomino.com

Elise Øverland
© Elise Øverland (pp 100–105)
www.eliseoverland.com

Felder Felder
© Arved Colvin-Smith (pp 106)
© Indigital Media (pp 109–115)
Customized underwear: Felder Felder for Triumph (pp 111, 115)
www.felderfelder.com

Graeme Armour
© Graeme Armour (pp 116–123)
www.graemearmour.com

Ilaria Nistri
© Gilardo Gallo (pp 125, 126–129, 134, 136–137)
© Federica Di Giovanni (pp 130–133)
© Ilaria Nistri (p 135)
www.ilarianistri.com

Jade Kang
© Jade Kang (pp 138–147)
www.kangst.com

Joanna Kulpa
© Evaan Kheraj (p 148)
© Trevor Brady (pp 150–151, 155)
© David Macgillivray (pp 152–153)
www.kulpa.ca

Jonathan Cohen
© Evan Miller (pp 156–163)
www.jonathancohencollection.com

Karolin Kruger
© Christoph Schemel (pp 164–171)
www.karolinkruger.com

Katie Gallagher
© Katie Gallagher (pp 174–183)
www.katiegallagher.com

Kilian Kerner
© Corina Lecca (pp 184–188, 190–193)
© Katja Kuhl (p 189)
www.kiliankerner.de

Kristofer Kongshaug
© Kristofer Kongshaug (pp 194–201)
www.kristoferkongshaug.com

Krystof Strozyna
© Krystof Strozyna (pp 202–207)
www.krystofstrozyna.com

Lako Bukia
© Simon Armstrong (pp 208–213, 216–217)
© Laboratory Nakanimamasakhlisi (p 214)
www.lakobukia.com

Limi Feu
© limi feu (pp 218–225)
www.limifeu.com

Mandy Coon
© Samantha Rapp (pp 226, 231–237)
© Sean Brackbill (pp 228–229)
www.mandycoon.com

Marko Mitanovski
© Christopher Dadey (pp 238, 244–245)
© Anne-Marie Michel (p 241)
© SHOWstudio (p 242)
© Marko Sovilj (p 243)
www.markomitanovski.com

Mary Katrantzou
© Chris Moore (pp 246–255)
www.marykatrantzou.com

Matteo Thiela
© Co Studio and Filippo Mutani (pp 256–263)
www.matteothiela.it

Orschel-Read
© Paul Morgan (pp 264, 268 L, 269 L, 271)
© Peter Ashworth (pp 268 R, 269 R)
© Christopher Dadey (pp 272–273)
www.orschel-read.com

Park Choon Moo
© Dan and Corinna Lecca (pp 274–279)
© Park Choon Moo (pp 280–285)
www.parkchoonmoo.com

Perret Schaad
© Perret Schaad (pp 286–295)
www.perretschaad.com

Rad Hourani
© Rad Hourani Inc. (pp 296–309)
www.radhourani.com

Risto
© Dan and Corinna Lecca (pp 310–319)
www.ristobimbiloski.com

Ronald Abdala
© Ronald Abdala Ltd (pp 320–331)
www.ronaldabdala.com

Siki IM
© Isa Asha Penzlien (pp 332–343)
www.sikiim.com

Silvio Betterelli
© Graziano Ferrari (pp 344–355)
www.silviobetterelli.it

Steffie Christiaens
© Shoji Fuji (pp 356–365)
www.steffiechristiaens.com

TÔ Long-Nam
© Mark Pillai (pp 366–375)
www.tolongnam.com

Yotam Solomon
© WireImage Michael Bezjian (pp 376, 380–383)
© Odessy Barbu (p 379)
www.yotamsolomon.com

Young Li-Lee
© Lilee (pp 384–393)
www.li-lee.com

332255 ✓

BACKSTAGE PASS

BARTON PEVERIL
COLLEGE LIBRARY
EASTLEIGH SO50 5ZA

CONCEPT BY
RALF DAAB

CATWALK DESIGNED BY
MEIRÉ UND MEIRÉ

DIRECTED BY
PATRICE FARAMEH

STAGE LAYOUT BY
NATHALIE GROLIMUND

PRODUCTION MANAGEMENT
CHRISTIANE BLASS

BIOS AND INTERVIEWS BY
NICKY STRINGFELLOW

PRODUCED BY

FARAMEHMEDIA.COM
NEW YORK CITY

PUBLISHED AND DISTRIBUTED
WORLDWIDE BY

WWW.DAAB-MEDIA.COM
SCHEIDTWEILERSTR. 69 · 50933
COLOGNE GERMANY

PRINTED WITH CARE
IN ITALY BY
GRAFICHE FLAMINIA

GRAFICHEFLAMINIA.COM

ISBN 978-3-942597-15-9

JOIN OUR COMMUNITY AND
PRESENT YOUR WORK TO A
WORLDWIDE AUDIENCE

WWW.EDAAB.COM

© 2011 DAAB MEDIA GMBH All rights reserved. No part of this publication may be reproduced or transmitted in any form or by any means, electronic or mechanical, including photocopy, recoarding or any information storage and retrieval system, without permission in writing from the copyright owner(s).